JOURNAL OF ARMORED ASSAULT & HELIBORNE WARFARE

VOL.18

7818

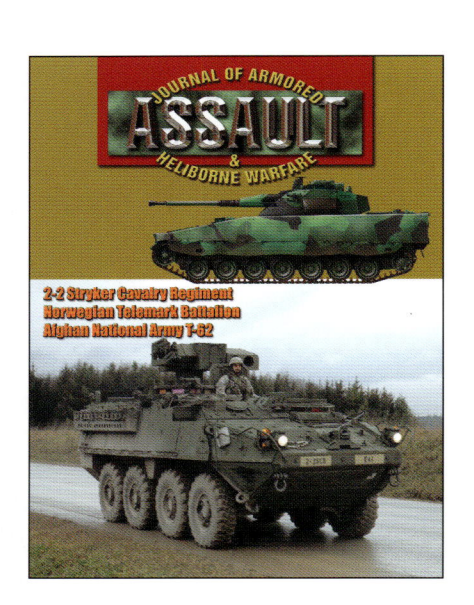

Cougar Steel
FTX of the 2nd Squadron, 2nd Stryker Cavalry Regiment
Ralph Zwilling — p3

NORWAY'S TELEMARK BATTALION
Yves Debay — p26

Afghanistan's Battleweary T-62 Tanks
3rd Tank Kandak
Yves Debay — p41

Copyright © 2007
by CONCORD PUBLICATIONS CO.
10/F, B1, 603-609 Castle Peak Road
Kong Nam Industrial Building
Tsuen Wan, New Territories,
Hong Kong
www.concord-publications.com

All rights reserved. No part of this publication may be reproduced, stored in a retrieval system or transmitted in any form or by any means, electronic, mechanical, photocopying or otherwise, without the prior written permission of Concord Publications Co.

We welcome authors who can help expand our range of books. If you would like to submit material, please feel free to contact us.

We are always on the look-out for new, unpublished photos for this series. If you have photos or slides or information you feel may be useful to future volumes, please send them to us for possible future publication. Full photo credits will be given upon publication.

ISBN 962-361-136-6
printed in Hong Kong

Cougar Steel
FTX of the 2nd Squadron, 2nd Stryker Cavalry Regiment
Ralph Zwilling

Eagle Company commander Captain Gentile's M1126 Stryker ICV. Each rifle company headquarters fields two ICVs. Note the Cougar marking in front of the first wheel and the lifting eyes used to lift the vehicle for shipping and maintenance.

The night is starlit and very quiet when the infantry soldiers of the 2nd Squadron, 2nd Stryker Cavalry Regiment, all equipped with AN/PVS-7D or AN/PVS-14 night vision goggles, slowly walk down a muddy trail on the outskirts of Riyahd in the Iraqi province of Salah ad Din to get into position for tonight's mission. Reliable intelligence sources reported that Abu Qasim, a high value target, should be in the two story building taking part in a meeting with several other insurgents. The 30 soldiers are armed with M4A1 carbines, M249 Squad Automatic Weapons, M203A1 grenade launchers and a M24 Sniper Weapon System. Their four M1126 Stryker Infantry Carrier Vehicles (ICV) will provide cal.50 machine gun and 40mm grenade fire support if necessary, but right now they quietly scan their surroundings with the Thermal Imagine Modules of their Kongsberg Remote Weapon Stations. In the event of possible casualties, the crew of a M1133 Stryker Medical Evacuation Vehicle is stationed behind one of the ICVs. If necessary, the infantry platoon could also call for 120mm mortar fire support from the four M1129 Mortar Carrier Vehicles already in firing position a few kilometres east of town. Everything it well prepared for tonight's raid. Quietly the soldiers get closer to the building and prepare to breach the entrance door with a C4 explosive strap. While an engineer sets the strap's fuze, the nine soldier entry force waits in single file around the corner. A loud explosion signals that the large metal door is open and the soldiers immediately enter the rooms with rifle mounted Surefire flashlights illuminating the darkness. In less then 120 seconds the soldiers cleared every room in the building and arrested Abu Qasim along with two other insurgents who are accused of building Improvised Explosive Devices (IEDs). Some of their IEDs recently killed two U.S. soldiers while driving in their up-armored M1114 HMMWV on Main Supply Route (MSR) Red. Without wasting time and using the effects of their surprise raid, they check the entire house for hidden weapons and explosives. The soldiers find an additional four civilians in the kitchen who are arrested and transported back to Forward Operating Base (FOB) Cougar, located 25 minutes away, for further identification and questioning. To prevent attack by other insurgents or members of the New Iraqi Guard, the soldiers want to minimize the time spent conducting the raid. Within only 20 minutes the soldiers completed the raid, arrested the High Value Target (HVT) and two other insurgents, arrested four civilians and also searched the building confiscating four AK-47 rifles and eight 81mm mortar rounds which are used to build the deadly IEDs. While this operation sounds like it is being conducted in Iraq, this raid was part of a Field Training Exercise held by the 2nd Squadron "Cougar" at a training area in Bavaria, Germany.

A M1126 Stryker Infantry Carrier Vehicle of Eagle Company pulling security at the outskirts of Zaab. The ICV is an armored personnel carrier that in addition to a two-man crew transports a nine-man infantry squad in its 11m³ troop compartment. The vehicle is the primary weapon system of the Stryker Brigade Combat Team (SBCT) which can field a total of 127 M1126 Stryker ICVs.

While Eagle Company soldiers, police and Iraqi Security Forces conducted another foot patrol through Zaab, the ISF commander was killed by a well-aimed shot near the market place and police station. This action caused the remaining ISF soldiers to quit working with the U.S. soldiers and leave town.

Before searching the houses located around the market place for hidden weapons and suspicious persons who could have killed the ISF commander, soldiers of 2nd Platoon bring the body of the dead ISF commander to the temporary observation post near the mosque. Note the mix of ACU and Woodland camouflaged equipment.

The 2nd Squadron's Road to War

The Field Training Exercise scenario Cougar Steel, conducted from 4 to 14 December 2006 at the Grafenwöhr Training Area in southern Germany, was based on the current situation in Iraq where the government, lead by Prime Minister Nouri al-Maliki, continues to seek stability and security in a country with violent Sunni and Shia Insurgency and terrorist elements. As they attempt to establish a safe and stable environment, the Iraqi Security Forces still have problems securing the country independently of assistance from Coalition Forces. Given this fact, the Field Training Exercise (FTX) of the 2nd Squadron, 2nd Stryker Cavalry Regiment (2-2 SCR) was conducted to prepare the squadron to operate in that environment.

The 2-2 SCR road to war began in November 2006 when Sunni rejectionists, calling themselves the New Republican Guard (NRG), used cached weapons, materials and agents within the Iraqi National Army in the Salah ad Din province to seize armored vehicles and overthrow the current military leadership within the province. The New Republican Guard began attacking weaker Iraqi National Army outposts and police stations in Salah ad Din, leading to a severe breakdown of law and order within several major Iraqi cities which the Iraqi Security Forces couldn't handle. Furthermore, Iraqi insurgents and terrorist elements supportive of the New Republican Guard assisted in attacking military, government, and law enforcement targets within the province. At the request of the Iraqi government, the Multi National Corps Iraq (MNCI) deployed the 2nd Stryker Cavalry Regiment to the Salah ad Din province in order to defeat the New Republican Guard as well as insurgent and terrorist elements **(Graphic 1)**. Based on reliable intelligence information, the NRG consists of numerous former military personnel, therefore, the NRG structure, doctrine and order of battle resembles that of former Warsaw Pact doctrine. Recently, New Republican Guard battalions (1-202 NRG Battalion and the 2-202 NRG Battalion) appeared in the vicinity of the Salah ad Din province where they operated primarily in the western region of the 2 SCR Area of Operations (AO). The Fedayeen, established as a paramilitary group beginning in 1995 by Saddam Hussein and the Ba`athist regime, have been training on special operations tactics and started to operate well forward of the NRG. The Sunni insurgents saw these developments in the province as their opportunity to rise up with both the NRG and Fedayeen and cause a greater upheaval within the current government. The increase of Sunni insurgents and Fedayeen operating in the Salah ad Din province has not only been noted near the cities of Ad Duluiyah and Tariq Sooq, but also to the east in Suliyamaniyah and Kirkuk.

Graphic 1

This Staff Sergeant provides cover for his comrades removing the body of the dead ISF commander. Like many 2nd SCR soldiers, this NCO is equipped with a mix of ACU and Woodland camouflaged equipment. He is armed with a 5.56mm M4A1 carbine fitted with a M68 Close Combat Optic (CCO) and an AN/PEQ-2A aiming light and a Surefire flashlight. The M68 CCO aiming dot's brightness is adjustable for better visibility and increased battery life.

A four-man infantry team prepares to enter a house in Zaab in order to search for hidden weapons and explosives. Based on their intelligence reports, the Eagle soldiers believed that the Mansourian Insurgent teams operating in the vicinity of Zaab and Riyadh had the capability to execute Suicide Vehicle Borne Improvised Explosive Device (SVBIED) and Vehicle Borne Improvised Explosive Devices (VBIED) attacks approximately once every 72 hours.

The mission of 2nd Squadron "Cougars" 2nd Cavalry Regiment, commanded by Lieutenant Colonel Reineke, was to conduct offensive operations to secure AO Cougar not later than 5 December 2006 in order to create a safe and secure environment and transition the Area of Responsibility back to the civil authorities or follow on forces. Decisive to the operation of the 2nd Squadron was the destruction of Anti-Iraqi Forces (AIF) cells in the city of Zaab to severely diminished their ability to influence the local populace. The commander's intend was as follows:

- Conduct stability operations to ensure the mutual compliance of Iraqi law and facilitate the Iraqi government's efforts to rebuild infrastructure.
- Rebuild legitimacy of local government and security forces.
- Conduct aggressive offensive operations in AO Cougar integrating lethal and non-lethal fires.
- Continue to develop Iraqi Security Forces.
- Control Main Supply Route (MSR) Red and Blue and the terrain dominating the major choke points along the MSRs.
- Minimize collateral damage.

For Operation Cougar Steel the motor pool of the 2nd Squadron, located at the northern edge of Rose Barracks in Vilseck Germany, was used as Forward Operating Base (FOB) Cougar. AO Nile located in the southeastern part of the Grafenwöhr Training Area (GTA) included a MOUT sight named Zaab with a mostly Sunni population. AO Thames was situated in the western portion of the training area and included MOUT sight Riyadh and Range 204, an anti-tank live fire range. The northern part of the GTA was named AO Rhine with the majority of operations being conducted at Ranges 307 and 311. The FTX was conducted in three phases; one infantry company secured AO Nile in order to create a safe and secure environment and to transition responsibility back to civil authorities or follow-on forces, the second infantry company secured AO Rhine to deny the enemy the ability to influence operations from the north, and the anti-armor company of the 2nd Stryker Cavalry Regiment conducted anti-armor ambushes to destroy enemy armor threats in AO Thames to protect the western flank of the regiment. The remaining infantry company was tasked to protect Logistical Package (LOGPAC) operations and provide a Quick Reaction Force (QRF) supporting the other two infantry companies **(Graphic 2)**. Given the high probability of IED attacks and small scale ambushes along roads and along the Main Supply Routes (MSRs), all ground assault convoys had to consist of at least three vehicles.

The road to war for the 2nd Squadron, 2nd Stryker Cavalry Regiment's exercise began in November 2006 when Sunni rejectionists, calling themselves the New Republican Guard (NRG), used cached weapons, materials and agents within the Iraqi National Army in the Salah ad Din province to seize armored vehicles and overthrow the current military leadership within the province. The NRG began attacking weaker Iraqi National Army outposts and police stations in Salah ad Din, leading to a severe breakdown of law and order within several major Iraqi cities which the Iraqi Security Forces couldn't handle. This photo shows an ISF soldier wearing the Desert Camouflage Uniform (DCU) jacket and being armed with a M4A1 carbine with AN/PEQ-2A aiming light, M68 CCO and a forward hand grip.

Phase I (Initial Entry) began on 5 December 2006 with Fox Company securing AO Rhine and Dog Company securing AO Nile and lasted until 7 December. Eagle Company was held in reserve and provided the QRF.

Phase II (Steady State) lasted from 8 to 10 December with Dog Company securing AO Rhine and Eagle securing AO Nile while Fox Company provided the QRF.

Phase III (Transition) started on 11 December with Eagle Company securing AO Rhine and Fox Company securing AO Nile. During this phase Dog Company performed the QRF mission. This phase ended on 14 December with the conditions set for a successful transfer of authority between 2nd Squadron, 2nd Stryker Cavalry Regiment and Iraqi Security Forces throughout AO Cougar.

Graphic 2

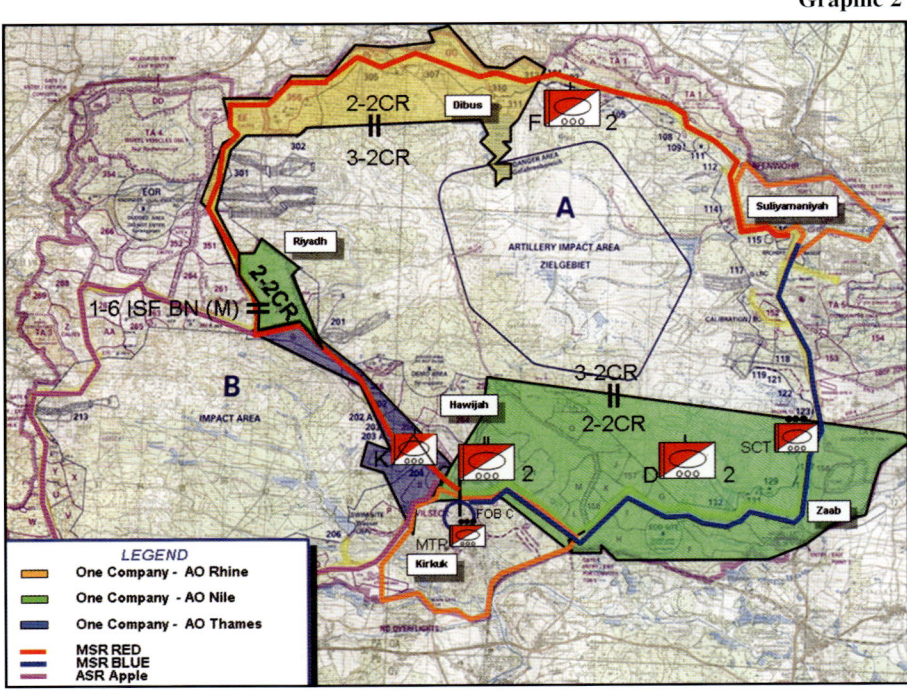

This young ISF soldier is armed with a 5.56mm M4A1 carbine with an attached 40mm M203A1 grenade launcher and a M68 CCO. He wears a Desert Camouflage Uniform (DCU) with the cut of the new ACU. Nearly 10,000 prototype uniforms were issued to soldiers of the 3rd Brigade, 2nd U.S. Infantry Division, the first operational Stryker Brigade Combat Team. In November 2003 the unit deployed to Iraq where the new design was tested under combat conditions. At that time the uniform was still in the desert camouflage pattern also used by the Desert Combat Uniform.

The regimental anti-armor company "Killer", normally attached to 2-2 SCR, remained in AO Thames for the duration of the entire FTX.

The key tasks of the maneuver units included the identification and conduct of bilateral negotiations with local key leaders, the safeguard of key municipal and religious leaders, conduct of **S**ewage, **W**ater **E**nergy, **A**cademic, **T**raining, **M**edical, **S**ecurity (SWEAT-MS) assessments and the protection of key infrastructure. The battalion mortar platoon conducted counter fire operations, offensive fire operations and also served as the squadron's Quick Reaction Force. The reconnaissance platoon performed area and route reconnaissance, security operations, performed squadron ORF missions and supported company operations with sniper sections. During the entire FTX Cougar Steel, the Tactical Command Post (TOC) and the ALOC (Army Logistic Operations Center) were located in FOB Cougar. The squadron's dining facility, aid station and the maintenance point were also located at the FOB.

After successful completion of operations in the province; all anti-Iraqi forces (AIF) were killed or arrested, infrastructure was secured, and the 2nd Squadron returned operational responsibility of the Area of Operations back to the Iraqi Security Forces before redeploying to its home station in Vilseck, Germany.

For easier identification during Field Training Exercise Cougar Steel, Kurdish Police officers wore Woodland uniforms, but were also armed with M4A1 carbines. As in Iraq, most of the police officers or ISF soldiers cover their face to prevent identification by insurgents. Note the Picatinny handguard that replaces the weapon's stock handguard allowing the user to mount a variety of accessories.

With the Eagles in Salah ad Din

At approximately 1530h on 8 December 2006, the 2nd Platoon of Eagle Company, led by Captain Gentile and 1LT Naparstek, entered the outskirts of Zaab, a MOUT site located at the Grafenwöhr Training Area, to secure the city and end the insurgency and constant violence. Their first objective was to contact the doctor of the local hospital, the Imam and Mayor Fawzi Ahmed Khalif to establish an initial meeting and create a base for future cooperation and support by coalition forces. In recent days the stability in the Sunni-dominated town had continued to decline as hostilities against

The infantry rifle squad has nine soldiers; the squad leader, two fire team leaders, two automatic riflemen, two riflemen and two grenadiers. Their armament consists of five 5.56mm M4A1 carbines, two M4A1 carbines with 40mm M203A1 grenade launchers and two 5.56mm M249 Squad Automatic Weapons.

This Eagle Company gunner is armed with a 7.62mm M240B machine gun and is assigned to the company's weapons squad which consists of a squad leader and two 3-man machine gun teams. It provides the primary base for the platoon's rifle squads maneuver with highly accurate short and long range direct and small-arms fires against enemy personnel and equipment.

Questioning Zaab's inhabitants didn't produce any new information, but after an hour Eagle soldiers positively identified a local man when his hands turned red after spraying them with a fluid reacting with gunpowder. While one soldier conducts a detailed body search, his comrade pulls security with a 5.56mm M4A1 carbine.

coalition forces in other Sunni-dominated areas had taken a sharp rise. Additionally, the migration of numerous Kurdish families and the fact that both the police chief and the Imam were Kurds, while the mayor was a Sunni, had started ethnic conflicts with the local Sunni population. This situation had the potential to become increasing volatile as the date for Saddam Hussein's execution approached. Although a curfew from 2000h to 0700h was announced, it had not been adhered to by the local population due to the lack of Iraqi Security Forces (ISF) or Iraqi Police (IP) or their willingness to enforce it. The current situation showed once again that the ISF and IP were unable to provide security in the province without the help of coalition forces.

The situation in Zaab lead 2-2 SCR to send Eagle Company into AO Nile in order to secure Zaab and provide a safe environment for the inhabitants. Another hot spot was Riyadh, located approximately 45 minutes to the west, which was controlled by another infantry platoon from Captain Gentile's company. When the combat patrol left their vehicles at 1535h, an ISF soldier accidentally discharged his rifle causing confusion and trouble with the Iraqi population which thought they were being attacked by the U.S. and ISF soldiers. As a consequence of this action, Mayor Fawzi Ahmed Khalif refused to let the company establish a command post in the city of Zaab. Instead, he only offered them an old tumbledown shack located 1km north of town for their observation post, and stated he didn't want to see soldiers in the town. Since continued conversations between

On the afternoon of 9 December 2nd Platoon was relieved by the 1st Platoon lead by 1LT Santarosa and ordered to pull security in Zaab for the following 24 hours. The water-cooled Caterpillar 6-cylinder 3126 I6 JP8/diesel engine with 7.2-liter displacement, exhaust turbocharger, inter-cooling and a Hydraulically-actuated Electronically-controlled Unit Injector (HEUI), provides the 18.3 ton vehicle a maximum speed of 101 km/h.

Depending on mission requirements, the RWS can be fitted with either a 40mm Mk19 MOD3 automatic grenade launcher or a 12.7mm M2 HB machine gun in its universal soft-mount cradle. It is also possible to mount a 7.62mm M240B machine gun with an adapter. Based on the manufacturer's specifications, the M151 RWS can be operated in temperatures ranging from – 40° C to + 65° C. Four M6 smoke grenade dischargers are fitted to the RWS. Each M6 has four 66 mm barrels that can be fired simultaneously or individually.

When 1LT Santarosa was finally able to contact the old Imam, he refused to speak with the young U.S. officer and insisted he would only speak with the Cougars' chaplain. An infantry squad, let by Staff Sergeant Hopkins, escorted Chaplain Botsford and his assistant, Sergeant Pena, to the entrance of the mosque where they spoke with the Imam making sure he understood that U.S. forces were in Zaab to establish security and would not leave until the job was accomplished. Note that the chaplain covered the cross on his body armor with green tape as some Muslims feel offended by the cross.

Captain Gentile and the mayor didn't produce success, the 2nd Platoon had no other choice but to occupy the old shack even though this kept them from contacting the Imam and the doctor. Because of the unfortunate accident, U.S. soldiers were not able to begin building a trusting relationship with the local leaders and offer them support in the form of medicine, food or construction materials.

Immediately after establishing their temporary observation post, the young platoon leader sent a foot patrol consisting of seven soldiers to scout the surrounding area making sure there were not insurgents or hidden Improvised Explosive Devices (IEDs). At 1805h a sniper team identified suspicious people armed with weapons outside the old mosque. Shortly after receiving this information, 1LT Naparstek ordered his infantry soldiers and a truck with ISF soldiers supported by two M1126 Stryker ICVs to the town center. Due to the insurgents` heavy small arms fire, they couldn't get close to the mosque, but had to return to the observation post on the outskirts of town. After reorganizing the patrol, 2nd Platoon made another attempt to enter the town at 1830h with the intent of arresting the suspects. Approximately 30 minutes later, the Stryker soldiers approached the area around the mosque, occupied a nearby two story building and arrested two Iraqi men suspected of firing small arms. After establishing 360° security around the house, 1LT Naparstek tried once again to contact the doctor of the hospital and the local Kurdish police chief. Mayor Fawzi Ahmed Khalif was not at the scene as he had already left Zaab in the afternoon for a meeting with some sheiks in Riyadh. The following night was predominately quiet with 2nd Platoon soldiers conducting several patrols in and around Zaab, but without managing to find and arrest any additional insurgents.

While the Stryker soldiers, police and Iraqi Security Forces conducted another foot patrol through Zaab, the ISF commander was killed by a well-aimed shot near the market place and police station at 1226h. This action caused the remaining ISF soldiers to quit working with the U.S. soldiers and leave town. Now the platoon leader could only rely on the local police chief to help him find the assassins and establish security and stability in the Sunni town. Shortly after the attack, the Stryker soldiers and the Kurdish police officers searched all houses located around the market place for hidden weapons and suspicious persons who could have killed the ISF commander. Questioning of most of the inhabitants didn't bring any new information, but after an hour Eagle soldiers positively identified a local man when his hands turned red after spraying them with a fluid that reacts with gunpowder. The colour on the hands of the young Iraqi was 100% proof that he had recently fired a weapon. After a long tactical questioning by the U.S. platoon leader, he admitted killing the ISF commander for working with the new Iraqi government. In the end, the criminal was arrested by the Eagle soldiers and handed over to the Iraqi Police.

After conducting another foot patrol, at approximately 1420h 2nd Platoon was relieved by the 1st Platoon lead by 1LT Santarosa and ordered to pull security in Zaab for the following 24 hours. The leaders of both platoons visited the doctor asking if he needed support and requesting he help speak with the Imam and local inhabitants. When the doctor wanted to speak with a medically trained person, the platoon leaders ordered a combat medic to the hospital. During the resulting conversation, the combat medic donated some medical supplies to the doctor. When the platoon was finally able to contact the old Imam he refused to speak with the young U.S. officers and insisted he would only speak with the Cougars` chaplain. An infantry squad, let by Staff Sergeant Hopkins, escorted Chaplain Botsford and his assistant, Sergeant Pena, to the

The Stryker's ammunition basic load includes either 2,000 rounds of 12.7mm ammunition for the M2 HB machine gun or 480 40mm grenades for the Mk19 MOD3 automatic grenade launcher as well as sixteen 66mm smoke grenades. The 12.7mm or 40mm ammunition boxes are normally stored in the large stowage racks along the side of the upper hull or on the roof between the squad leader and air guard hatches.

For FTX Cougar Steel the 2nd Squadron motor pool, located at the northern edge of Rose Barracks in Vilseck, Germany was used as Forward Operating Base (FOB) Cougar and protected by gate guards. Note the Petzl light attached to the soldier's Advanced Combat Helmet (ACH). His M4A1 carbine is fitted with an AN/PEQ-2A aiming light, M68 CCO and a Surefire flashlight.

This M1129 Stryker Mortar Carrier Vehicle Version B (MCV-B) of Eagle Company was seen at the outskirts of Zaab. The mortar section is the rifle company's primary indirect fire support element. The section consists of ten soldiers organized into two mortar crews each equipped with a 120mm mortar mounted on a M1129 Stryker MCV-B allowing for rapid and flexible delivery of indirect fires and increased responsiveness through rapid maneuver in support of company operations. Both crews are also equipped with a 60mm M224 Lightweight Company Mortar System which enables the section to provide a more lightweight dismounted mortar system to meet the requirements of a traditional light infantry mission.

entrance of the mosque where they spoke with the Imam making sure he understood that U.S. forces were in Zaab to establish security and would not leave until the job was accomplished. Chaplain Botsford is a dynamic person with the ability to solve difficult problems between different cultures or religions. As a result, the meeting between the chaplain and the Imam was very open and successful and the tense situation in Zaab relaxed a little bit. In the afternoon, the mayor returned to Zaab and became very angry concerning the U.S. forces occupation of the building beside the mosque. The platoon leader needed all of his persuasive power to ease the mayor's mind.

Based on their intelligence reports, the Eagle soldiers believed that the Mansourian Insurgent teams operating in the vicinity of Zaab and Riyadh had the capability to execute Suicide Vehicle Borne Improvised Explosive Device (SVBIED) and Vehicle Borne Improvised Explosive Devices (VBIED) attacks approximately once every 72 hours. Given this fact, they checked every car for possible booby traps and hidden explosives. They also knew that the insurgents recently moved a mortar cell into the Area of Operations targeting FOB Cougar from time to time and causing some casualties among the coalition soldiers. Furthermore, the insurgents influenced the civilians working for coalition forces through coercion and intimidation to obtain information on the squadron and activities in and around Zaab. Reports coming from two unconfirmed sources had stated that Mahmoud Yousef Abd Al Tikriti, Mohammed Abdullah Ahmed Al Jabouri and Abu Said frequently travelled through AO Cougar. All three individuals were on the MNCI High Value Target List (HVTL). Al Jabouri was reported to have a house in downtown Zaab, so Stryker soldiers maintained a watchful eye for him when patrolling the city. During the night of 9 to 10 December, 1st Platoon arrested and killed two of the High Value Targets. A problem which the platoon leader had to solve was the arrest of Mohammed Al Jabouri. Al Jabouri hid in the mosque, which U.S. soldiers were not permitted to enter, but was immediately arrested and interrogated when he left this hiding-place at the crack of dawn.

When Eagle Company finished the training in AO Nile on 11 December, it moved to Range 307 located in AO Rhine in the northern part of the training area. The three infantry platoons trained in conducting raids supported by M1126 Stryker Infantry Carrier Vehicles and an engineer squad equipped with a M1132 Stryker Engineer Squad Vehicle during the next three days. Each platoon began the first day of training with a dry-fire exercise at 1000h followed by an exercise with blank ammunition at 1230h. At 1500h the platoons conducted the raid with live ammunition. To build proficiency in night operations, the platoon conducted a raid with blank ammunition at 1830h to get familiar with the situation followed by another run at 2200h with live rounds. The training scenario conducted at Range 307 was as follows.

Eagle Company 2-2 SCR received intelligence information that there were several High Value Targets in a house located on the outskirts of Dibus in the province of Salah ad Din consisting of Kurds and Sunni inhabitants. A two man sniper team together with a dismounted Fire Support NCO (FSNCO) infiltrated the area to gain more details about the building and the environment. On order of Captain Gentile, two M1126 Stryker Infantry Carrier Vehicles (ICV) left the Tactical Assembly Area (TAA) and moved into Support by Fire Position 1 (SBF 1) where they opened fire on targets appearing at ranges up to 1.500m. With the first two vehicles in over-watch, another two Infantry Carrier Vehicles, M1132 Engineer Squad Vehicle, and M1133 Medical Evacuation Vehicle moved forward to SBF 2 where they picked up the sniper team and FSNCO. Once the second team was established in SBF 2, the first two Strykers moved 500m forward from SBF 1 to SBF 3. The second team then drove on a parallel road to SBF 4. Shortly after arriving at this position, the weapons squad, snipers and FSNCO dismounted from the Stryker armored vehicles which were already firing with their cal.50 machine guns and 40mm grenade launchers. As soon as the dismounted soldiers established a proper firing position close to the vehicles, they also opened fire with their two 7.62mm M240B machine guns and the 7.62mm M24 Sniper Weapon System (SWS). The trail to the insurgents' hideout was blocked with a booby trapped concertina wire obstacle, therefore, the engineer Stryker moved forward to SBF 4 and five engineers immediately dismounted. The engineers used a long Bangalore

The squadron's Tactical Operations Center (TOC) was established in the middle of FOB Cougar. Personnel from the S3 section, S2 section, and the fires cell habitually man the squadron's TOC along with an augmenting United States Air Force (USAF) Tactical Air Control Party (TACP) section and other supporting elements such as combat engineers, military intelligence, or air defenders. The M1113 HMMWVs are equipped with S-832/G shelters.

Photos from inside the squadron Tactical Operations Center are very rare. Note the rack with the three flat screens showing TV images on the left, FBCB2 information in the middle and current operations on the right. Most of the TOCs computers are IBM notebooks. The radios on the desks belong to the Tactical Operations Center Inter-Communication System (TOCNET) developed by Sanmina-SCI's Defense and Aerospace division. The system is ruggedized for harsh environments and has a network expandable to over 1,000 communication assets/channels.

torpedo with a time fuze to remove the wire obstacle and open a clear lane. To avoid injuries from the Bangalore, all dismounts returned to the protection of their armored vehicles when the fuze was set by the engineers. After the explosion cleared a lane through the obstacle, the engineers again dismounted, proofed the lane for unexploded ammunition and marked the lane for the following infantry soldiers. Without wasting time, the Stryker soldiers passed through the lane and moved forward to the building which was still being suppressed by the ICVs with machine gun and grenade launcher fire. First Squad was tasked to support the entry force by breaching the door with a strap consisting of C4 explosive. After blowing open the door, the infantry soldiers entered the building, searched the rooms one by one and killed or arrested all insurgents. Even though the Cougar soldiers conducted raids like this previously, they were reminded that the last soldier in line squeezes the man in front who passes the silent signal forward. When the first soldier in the line receives the signal he starts moving forward into the next room with all others in line following him. If the soldiers were to yell "go", instead of squeezing their comrades, the enemy would be warned of the coming entry force giving him the chance to open fire. In order to prevent friendly fire inside the very narrow and complex building, soldiers yelled a short password and would not enter the next building or the room until they heard the response from their comrades. Correctly walking up an open stairwell to the second floor based on standard operating procedures was a major objective of this training lane and one of the most dangerous tasks in an enemy occupied building. When moving up an open stairwell, the enemy can easily kill soldiers who do not use proper movement techniques and available cover. Senior NCOs and officers supervised all actions on the training lane and sometimes required certain training aspects be repeated if they weren't conducted 100% correct the first time. In the case of walking up the open stairwell, soldiers learned to use proper cover with the ability to respond to any enemy attack from all directions on the second floor. As soon as all floors were cleared, the soldiers hung signal panels on the outside of the front windows showing their comrades in the Infantry Carrier Vehicles that the building was completely occupied by U.S. forces. Finally, the soldiers had to identify all insurgents and remove all civilians from the building. After photographing all insurgents either dead or alive, and ensuring there were no insurgent weapons, explosives or documents left in the building, the infantry soldiers left the house as fast as they approached. When leaving the building the soldiers on the second floor left the building first followed by the soldiers in the first floor. Once out of the building, the soldiers quickly moved back to their Stryker vehicles which were still providing security at Support by Fire positions 3 and 4. The entire training lane took between 90 and 120 minutes depending on the skill of the infantry platoon and the weather and light conditions at the time. The objective of this training lane was to

The Tactical Operations Center Inter-Communication System can be configured to meet the unit's specific communication requirements. The portable desktop Crew Access Unit (CAU) includes a headset and two ANR or non-ANR headsets ports. This TOCNET operator was seen at the ALOC (Administrative/Logistics Operations Center) located at the outskirts of FOB Cougar.

Each rifle company also receives a Fire Support Team (FIST) from the HHC's Fire Support Platoon consisting of the Fire Support Officer, Fire Support NCO, Fire Support Specialist, Radio Telephone Operator and driver. It is equipped with the M1131 Stryker FSV providing combat laser designation capability for delivery of precision artillery or aerial-delivered munitions. Note the COM201B lightweight VHF and UHF communications antenna placed on top of the FSV.

The FIST assists the company commander in planning, integrating, coordinating, and executing all types of available supporting fires during tactical operations. Furthermore, the FIST is the commander's primary fire support coordinator and provides the commander a direct link to battalion indirect fire support systems. This M1131 Stryker FSV has additional armor plates fitted to the commander's cupola.

The 2nd Squadron, 2nd Stryker Cavalry Regiment

Let's take a closer look at the 2nd Squadron "Cougars" of the 2nd Stryker Cavalry Regiment. It consists of a Headquarters and Headquarters Company, three identically organized rifle companies (Dog, Eagle and Fox) and an attached regimental anti-armor company, "Killer" (**Graphic 3**). The 2nd Squadron's primary mission is to close with and destroy the enemy during full-spectrum operations through close, violent combat and counter-attacks. It is capable of accomplishing all missions historically identified with the infantry and is organized and equipped to conduct operations in all types of terrain and climatic conditions. The squadron can deploy rapidly and can be sustained by an austere support structure. It conducts operations against conventional and unconventional enemy forces and can function autonomously or as part of any combat brigade. The 2-2 SCR is a lethal force built around the infantryman. It possesses a robust array of direct and indirect fire systems to shape the battlespace and achieve decision in the close fight especially within restricted and severely restricted terrain. All the following information about the organization is based on the latest material developed by the U.S. Army Armor School at Fort Knox, Kentucky.

Graphic 3

conduct a raid supported by M1126 ICVs and M1132 ESVs rapidly and in accordance with standard operating procedures.

In addition to the already described training scenarios, Cougar Steel also included suicide vehicle borne IED attacks, IEDs, mortar and small arms attacks, kidnappings, demonstrations, complex ambushes and many more situations requiring the Cougar soldiers to use all their skills, knowledge and experience gained from previous exercises or deployments. The purpose of the Field Training Exercise was to train platoons on Platoon Critical Tasks both in a Situational Training Exercise (STX) and live fire environment. Although the FTX Cougar Steel was very realistic and forced each participating soldier to fulfil his role as he would in Iraq, this exerciser was just the beginning of a series of training exercises. The 2nd Squadron, 2nd Stryker Cavalry Regiment conducted company size training exercises in February 2007 at the Hohenfels Training Area located 60 kilometres south of the 2 SCR home station.

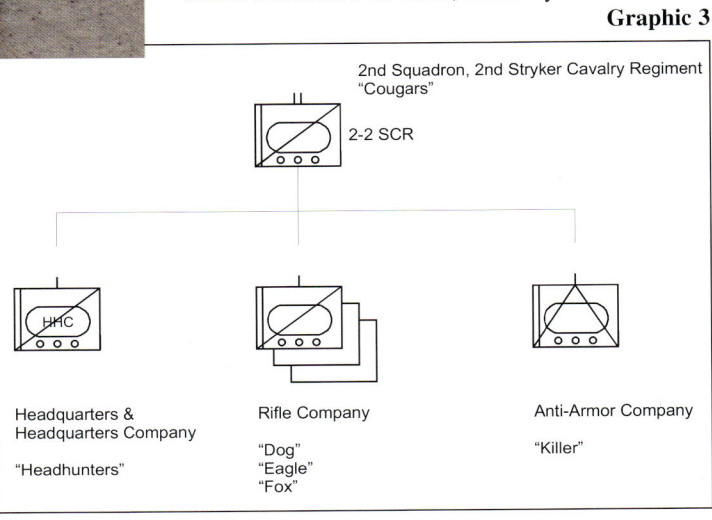

This Fire Support NCO operates the Remote Display Unit (RDU) which is connected to the Stand-alone Computer Unit (SCU) located at the rear of the vehicle. Note the Video Display Terminal (VDT) above the RDU. The VDT is linked to the Driver's Vision Enhancer, FBCB2 computer set, Remote Weapon's Station, vehicle diagnostic system, Embedded Training Module (ETM) and Interactive Electronic Technical Manual (IETM) providing situational awareness and information for the operator.

The M1131 Stryker FSV Command, Control, Communication, Computer, Intelligence, Surveillance and Reconnaissance equipment includes among others the Fire Support Sensor System (FS3) Mission Equipment Package (MEP) with attached Laser Designator Module (LDM), Forward Observer System (FOS), two AN/VRC-92F ASIP radios, a AN/VRC-88F radio, portable AN/PRC-119F ASIP radio, AN/UYK-128 FBCB2, AN/VSQ-2 (V) 1 EPLRS, Embedded Training Module, AN/PSN-11 PLGR and the Standalone Computer Unit (SCU) seen in this photo being connected with the Remote Display Unit (RDU).

The Headquarters & Headquarters Company "Headhunter" is divided into a squadron headquarters and the headquarters company. The squadron headquarters coordinates and controls all squadron activities and, therefore, consists of numerous different platoons, sections and squads. The Cougars are commanded by Lieutenant Colonel Reineke who forms the squadron command section together with the Executive Officer Major Soika and the Squadron Command Sergeant Major CSM Wood as well as their enlisted vehicle drivers. Their vehicles include a M1130 Stryker Commander's Vehicle (CV) and three HMMWVs.

The squadron staff consists of the personnel and administration section (S1), intelligence section (S2), operations section (S3), logistic section (S4), the communications section (S6) and the fires cell. The S1 section is equipped with a HMMWV, M1101 ¾ t cargo trailer, M1083A1 MTV truck and a M1095 MTV trailer, and is responsible for maintaining unit strength and conducting personnel actions. Furthermore, it identifies and reports critical personnel shortages to the commander and higher headquarters and it ensures assigned personnel transition smoothly into and out of the

The M1083A1 MTV 6x6 built by Stewart & Stevenson in West Sealy, Texas, is the primary cargo truck of the 2nd Stryker Cavalry Regiment. The 330hp 6-cylinder Caterpillar electronic controlled, fuel-injected JP-8/diesel engine with turbocharger and intercooling provides the 9.43 ton vehicle a maximum speed of 96km/h. The fuel tank holding 219 liters provides a maximum range of up to 483km. The MTV is equipped with a fully automatic Allison MD 3700SP transmission, electronic central tire inflation system and anti-lock braking system.

The Fire Support Sensor System (FS3) is a long-range multi-sensor system for the forward observer providing real-time ability to detect, recognize, identify and geo-locate targets. It enables Army forward observers to conduct 24-hour fire missions while remaining outside threat acquisition and engagement ranges. The FS3 provides precision far-target location and long-range target engagement incorporating an advanced second generation Forward-Looking Infrared (FLIR) sensor, an eye-safe laser rangefinder and a day TV camera with laser "see-spot" capability.

The 35,500 lb M1120 Load Handling System (LHS) produced by Oshkosh Truck Cooperation is a modified M977 HEMTT cargo truck redesigned to incorporate the OTC/Multi-fit LHS used on the Palletized Loading System (PLS). It's designed for rapid transport of all classes of supply with a payload capacity of 22,000 pounds. The vehicle is interoperable with NATO standard flatracks and air transportable in the C-130 Hercules aircraft. The M1120 LHS is powered by a 12.1-liter 8V92TA 8-cylinder Detroit Diesel engine with 450hp which is connected to an Allison HD4560P 6-speed automatic transmission. The fuel tank, holding 587 liters, provides a cruising range of up to 644km.

During FTX Cougar Steel, the 2 SCR anti-armor company conducted anti-armor ambushes to destroy enemy armor threats in AO Thames to protect the western flank of the regiment. This M1134 Stryker Anti-Tank Guided Missile (ATGM) vehicle was seen at Range 204 during live-fire. The Tube-launched, Optically-tracked Wire-command-link-guided (TOW) missile system has a maximum effective range of 3,750m. With the TOW-2B BGM-71F anti armor missile all known armor can be destroyed. The missile operates in a "flyover shoot down" top attack mode and features two explosively formed projectile warheads. The EFP warheads detonate simultaneously, one pointing downwards, the other slightly offset to give an increased hit probability.

squadron. During tactical operations, the S1 section operates together with the S4 section to provide Combat Service Support (CSS) to the squadron. This includes unit strength reporting to higher headquarters and coordination of unit replacements as directed by the squadron commander. Intelligence is one of the commander's most important decision-making tools. Therefore, the S2 section with its HMMWV and M1101 ¾ t cargo trailer is responsible for providing timely and accurate intelligence analysis and products in support of the commander, staff, and subordinate units. It supervises and coordinates collection, processing, production, and dissemination of intelligence in conjunction with the S3 section. The section makes analytical predictions on when and where battlefield actions will occur. It also provides analysis on the effects of the battlefield environment on friendly and enemy courses of action and capabilities. The S3 section is the commander's primary staff element for planning, coordinating, prioritizing, and synchronizing all squadron operations. The S3 vehicles include a M1130 Stryker CV, six HMMWVs, a HMMWV with an S-832/G shelter, a M1083A1 MTV truck, five trailers with PU-801 power generators, and two M1101 ¾ t cargo trailers. The operations section controls and directs the squadron's Tactical Operations Center (TOC) which acts as the control center for squadron tactical operations and coordinates critical support operations, as required, with the other staff sections. To ensure force protection and maintain survivability on the battlefield, it is capable of frequent, rapid displacement and is equipped with communications equipment with a low electronic signature. Personnel from the S3 section, S2 section, and the fires cell habitually man the squadron's TOC, along with an augmenting United States Air Force (USAF) Tactical Air Control Party (TACP) section and other supporting elements such as combat engineers, military intelligence, or air defenders. The S4 section is responsible for providing logistical planning and support to the squadron and operates the squadron's combat trains command post (CTCP). The S4 functions as the commander's primary logistics planner and provides timely and accurate logistical information required to support and sustain the individual maneuver companies with all classes of supply. The logistics section mans the CTCP in conjunction with elements of the S1 section and provides personnel and logistics reporting to higher headquarters. It also coordinates logistics resupply and unit replacements

Loading the twin-tube launcher is done manually through a large one-piece rear hatch in the roof of the rear compartment. While loading the launcher is elevated to +40°. To prevent the ASIP radio antennas being damaged by the blast of the TOW-2B ATGM, they can be automatically folded down. Note the two 5 Gallon fuel cans attached to the rear of the vehicle and the large storage baskets along the hull.

The elevated TOW system is mounted on the vehicle's roof between the two rear axles and slightly offset to the left. It consists of the elevation system, twin-tube missile launcher on the left, Modified Improved Target Acquisition System (MITAS) in the middle and four banks of smoke grenade launchers on the right side. The MITAS sensors are located in an armored enclosure with an armored door at the front protecting them from damage when not in use. The enclosure is centrally mounted on the elevation system. The MITAS includes the Target Acquisition System (TAS), Fire Control System and Battery Power Source. The TAS integrates a CCD TV direct view optic, second-generation FLIR Night Vision Sight (NVS), missile tracker, and an eye-safe laser rangefinder. MITAS enables target detection, acquisition and fire control during day or night and under all weather conditions. Both CCD TV day and FLIR NVS sights can be used in two fields of view; wide and narrow.

as required. Their vehicle park includes a HMMWV, a HMMWV with an S-832/G shelter and a M1101 ¾ t cargo trailer. The communications section provides the squadron with communications personnel capable of supporting squadron and company operations. The S6 section's signal officer is the primary planner for all communications and networking operations. He advises the commander, staff, and the maneuver companies on all network, signal, and communications matters. The communications section fields four HMMWVs, a HMMWV equipped with a S832/G shelter and AN/TYQ-120(V)1, two M1101 ¾ t cargo trailers, a trailer with a powerful PU-798 generator and a Satellite Transportable Terminal Trailer providing communication with other 2 SCR units via the Joint Network Node (JNN). The Joint Network Node-Network (JNN-N) is a suite of communications equipment, housed in transportable shelters and associated transit cases, providing the resources for the network manager to exercise effective control over communications links, trunks, and groups within the deployed network. The JNN-N provides the capability to interface those resources with satellite and terrestrial transmission resources to establish a robust network consistent with the Army's vision for the modular division and BCT force structure down to the squadron command post level. The JNN-N is comprised of five major field communications nodes, transit cases, and Ku band satellite transportable terminals for the division through squadron levels. The squadron's retransmission section has two M1098 HMMWVs with COMM 201 radio sets for FM radio retransmission. The fires cell consists of the fire support officer, a senior fire support NCO (FSNCO), an assistant FSNCO and one fire support specialist. It assists the squadron commander and S3 with planning, integrating, coordinating, and executing all types of available supporting fires during tactical operations as well as acting as the Squadron's primary civil affairs (non-lethal fires) cell. Furthermore it is the commander's primary fire support coordinator and provides a direct link to the squadron's indirect fire support systems and supporting artillery units. The fires cell fields a HMMWV and a HMMWV with an S-832/G shelter. Of course 2-2 SCR also has a unit ministry team (UMT) with a chaplain and his driver providing religious services and soldier welfare ministries. Finally there is a robust medical platoon offering the full spectrum of medical care. This platoon operates out the Squadron Aid Station (SAS).

The squadron's organic mortar platoon provides the most responsive indirect fires available to the squadron. The platoon's mission is to provide close and immediate fire support to the maneuver units. In addition to

As the M1128 Stryker Mobile Gun System (MGS) was only recently introduced into the U.S. Army on 15 May 2006, the MGS platoons of the 2nd Stryker Cavalry Regiment currently consist of two M1126 Stryker ICV and a M1134 Stryker Anti-Tank Guided Missile Vehicle (ATGM). In the future, all MGS platoons will be equipped with three M1128 Stryker MGS.

The regimental anti-armor company "Killer", normally attached to the 2nd Squadron, 2nd Stryker Cavalry Regiment, provides anti-tank fires as well as support to infantry assaults and destroy enemy bunkered in hard structures. The company is organized into a headquarters section, three anti-armor platoons, fire support platoon and a combat medic section. Each anti-armor platoon consists of three M1134 Stryker Anti-Tank Guided Missile Vehicles (ATGM) equipped with the TOW-2B ATGM and 7.62mm M240B machine gun.

The M1134 Stryker ATGM is based on the M1126 Stryker ICV, but instead of the Protector RWS is fitted with the Elevated TOW System. The ETS provides the vehicle with an effective long-range day and night capability to destroy enemy armor beyond the effective range of tank guns. Firing is only possible when the launcher is in the raised position and manually locked. In order to decrease the vehicle height for air transport, the ETS can be electrically lowered by 550mm.

supporting its parent squadron, the mortar platoon can support other units. The role of mortar units is to deliver deadly suppressive fires to support maneuver, especially against dismounted enemy infantry. Mortar units also fire smoke missions, mark targets, and provide point battlefield illumination. Mortar fires inhibit enemy fire and movement, allowing friendly forces to maneuver to a position of advantage. Effectively integrating mortar fires with dismounted maneuver is the key to successful combat at the rifle company and squadron level. The requirement to reduce collateral damage and non-combatant casualties requires precision fires and well-trained soldiers who understand the direct fire plan and who remain aware of the situation. The squadron's mortar platoon is organized into a platoon headquarters with two HMMWVs and two M1101 ¾ t cargo trailers and four mortar squads each with a M1129 Stryker Mortar Carrier Vehicle Version B (MCV-B) equipped with a 120mm Recoil Mortar System RMS6-L and a 81mm M252 Medium Extended Range Mortar. The 81mm mortar systems enable the mortar platoon to provide dismounted mortar support to the squadron during air assault and infiltration operations. The MCV-Bs improve the survivability of the mortar crew and equipment by providing increased flexibility, responsiveness, mobility, and protected transportation. The platoon's fire direction center (FDC) controls and directs the mortar platoon's maneuver and fires. With the addition of the mortar fire control system (MFCS), the squadron can potentially mass the effects of the two mortar platoon sections and the three company mortar sections, all under control of the mortar platoon HQ. The Fire Support Platoon has three M1131 Stryker Fire Support Vehicles (FSV) normally attached to the rifle companies.

The medical platoon provides unit-level medical support for the squadron. The medical platoon is responsible for providing Level I medical care. This care includes emergency medical treatment for wounds, injuries or illness, advanced trauma management, and sick call services. It also includes casualty collection and medical evacuation from the supported maneuver company to the squadron aid station (SAS). The medical platoon habitually establishes the SAS where it can best support the squadron. It normally operates under the direction of the squadron TOC and the CTCP. It is organized under a platoon headquarters with a HMMWV and M1102 1¼ t cargo trailer, a treatment squad, two medical evacuation squads and a combat medic section. The treatment squad has two M997 Maxi Ambulance vehicles, a HMMWV and three M1102 1¼ t cargo trailers. Each of the two medical evacuation squads have two M1133 Stryker Medical Evacuation Vehicles (MEV). The squadron reconnaissance platoon serves as the forward "eyes and ears" of the squadron commander. The primary mission of the reconnaissance platoon is to conduct mounted and dismounted reconnaissance to determine enemy composition and disposition along named areas of interest or targeted areas of interest. The platoon has one officer and 23 enlisted personnel. The platoon leader employs both the mounted and dismounted reconnaissance elements within the platoon. The reconnaissance platoon is organized into two sections of two M1127 Stryker Reconnaissance Vehicles (RV) each and three 5-man dismounted reconnaissance teams. These teams are divided between the platoon's two sections, with one "heavy" section transporting two reconnaissance teams and the other "light" team transporting one reconnaissance team and the platoon leader. The sniper squad has just one HMMWV and a M1101 ¾t cargo trailer and is a modular organization consisting of a squad leader and two identically equipped three-man sniper teams. Each team is capable of providing the squadron with a full range of sniper support and is equipped with both the 7.62mm M24 Sniper Weapon System (SWS) and the cal.50 M107 Long Range Sniper Rifle (LRSR). Additionally, the third member of the sniper team is armed with a 5.56mm M4A1 Carbine fitted with a 40mm M203A1 Grenade Launcher to provide protection and security for the sniper and his spotter as well as a means to break contact if the team is compromised. Squadron snipers are employed to support maneuver, kill essential enemy leadership or command personnel, disable lightly armored or "thin skinned" vehicles, enhance force protection, provide lethal accurate fires in urban operations and perform the counter-sniper role. The modularity of the sniper teams enables the augmentation of a sniper team to a subordinate company or task-

In addition to the Elevated TOW System, the M1134 Stryker ATGM is armed with a 7.62mm M240B machine gun providing 240° forward coverage and -20° to +60° of elevation. The M240B must be in the stowed position for the TOW-2B ATGM to fire. There are 10 boxes, each with 200 rounds of 7.62mm ammunition (M80 and M62 tracer linked) on board.

organization of a company sniper team to the squadron sniper squad for the execution of specific sniper missions.

The company headquarters section, equipped with two HMMWVs, two M1083A1 MTV trucks and two M1095 MTV trailers with 900 gallon water tanks, provides the immediate leadership, supply, and personnel support to all HHC personnel, including the squadron's command group, coordinating and special staff, and specialty platoons and squads. It includes the HHC commander, first sergeant, executive officer, and supporting supply and chemical sections. The United States Air Force Tactical Air Control Party (TACP) section has a M1130 Stryker CV which is usually manned by the Squadron S3 Air Officer, Joint Tactical Air Controllers (JTAC), a Fire Support Officer, vehicle commander and a driver. Their mission is to advise ground commanders on the best use of air power, establish and maintain command and control communications, control air traffic, act as an inter-service liaison and provide precision terminal attack guidance of U.S. and coalition close air support (CAS) and other air-to-ground aircraft **(Graphic 4)**.

The Fire Control System controls the missile flight and allows the gunner to lock onto the thermal image of a target. It also contains embedded training circuitry for sustained training and advanced built-in test equipment that provides a fault detection and isolation capability. The detachable ETS Gunner's Panel Assembly is mounted to the front of the gunner's seat which is situated in the vehicle's hull below the ETS and parallel to the commander's seat.

Graphic 4

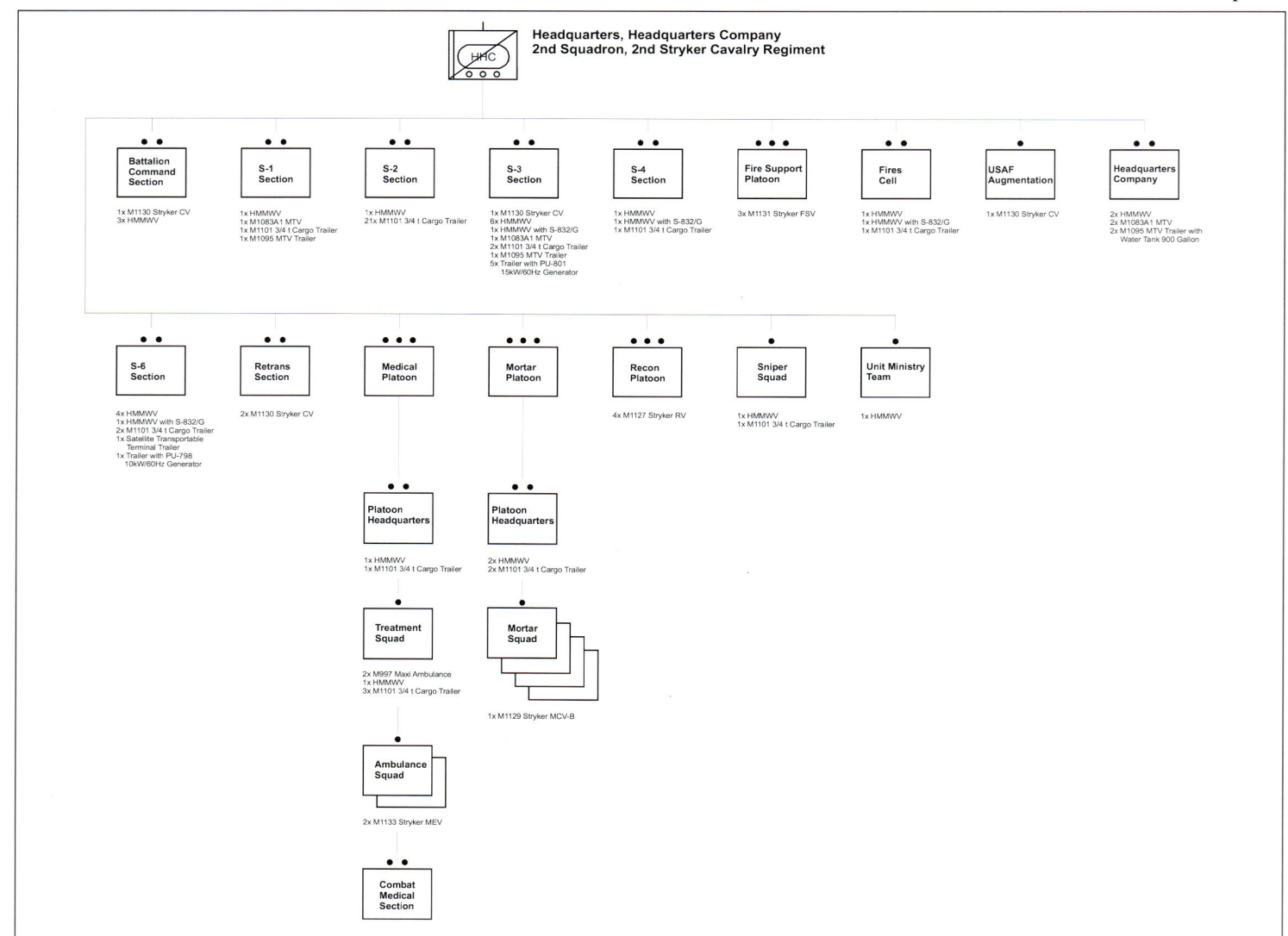

Private First Class Woodruff wears the new Army Combat Uniform (ACU) together with the Interceptor Body Armor (IBA) both in the Universal Digital Camouflage Pattern. Beginning in February 2005, the ACU became standard issue for all deployed troops and fielding to the entire Army is expected to be completed by December 2007. The U.S. Army claims that the new uniform provides enhanced functionality and ergonomics paired with providing one uniform deployable worldwide. Note the first aid pouch and the three magazine pouches attached to the IBA.

The vehicle commander's FBCB2 monitor is mounted to the left of the Video Display Terminal in the commander's direct field of view. Using FBCB2 and EPLRS, vehicle crews send and receive text messages, view maps and show satellite and air pictures. Vital tactical information gathered by reconnaissance assets can be displayed on digital maps and pictures showing the locations of mine fields and enemy positions. In addition, all vehicles in the surrounding area that have connectivity with the system are shown as small icons. The crew can insert information into the system through its own FBCB2 Blue Force Tracker terminal. The capability to quickly manage vital information provides the Stryker IAV crews with a superior situational awareness allowing them to conduct missions at high speed while maintaining a more accurate picture of both friendly and enemy forces.

The mission of the three rifle companies is to close with the enemy by means of fire and maneuver in order to destroy or capture him, repel his assaults by fire, close range combat and counterattack. The three rifle companies "Dog", "Eagle" and "Fox" are normally employed under the control of the squadron commander in the most forward part of the squadron's operational area. They fight as single elements or they are assigned missions for the subordinate platoons and squads. The company is supported by the squadron headquarters on a mission basis with 120mm and 81mm mortar fire, reconnaissance, medical, supply and transportation support. Each rifle company is organized into a company headquarters section, three rifle platoons, a mortar section, mobile gun system platoon, sniper team, fire support team and medical evacuation team.

The company headquarters section provides command, control and supervision of all organic and attached elements. It consists of the company commander, executive officer, first sergeant, company supply and NBC personnel, infantry carrier vehicle crews for the company commander and XO, and the Radio Telephone Operator (RATELO). Based on the new Modified Table of Organization and Equipment (MTOE), the company headquarters section fields two M1126 Stryker ICV, two HMMWVs, two M1083A1 MTV trucks, two M1101 ¾ t cargo trailers and two M1095 MTV trailers with 900 gallon water tanks. The rifle company commander, usually a captain, is responsible for training, maintenance and tactical employment of the company. In the field the first sergeant is responsible for overseeing administrative and logistic functions within the company such as re-supply and casualty evacuation operations while in garrison he is responsible for coaching, teaching and mentoring other NCOs within the company.

Each rifle platoon has a platoon headquarters, three rifle squads, a weapons squad and the mounted element consisting of the vehicle crews. The training and tactical employment of the rifle platoon is directed by the rifle platoon headquarters which is made up of the platoon leader, platoon sergeant, Radio Telephone Operator, Forward Observer and a Combat Medic. The rifle platoon is equipped with four M1126 Stryker ICV that provide rapid, protected, tactical and operational mobility of infantry squads to critical locations on the battlefield. Each ICV has a crew

Even though the Remote Weapon Station (RWS) is normally operated under armor, in case of a malfunction the vehicle commander can manually fire the cal.50 M2 HB machine gun. Note the two cables attached to the right upper hull as well as the water and fuel cans stored at the rear beside the ramp.

The two fuel tanks, located on both sides of the rear exterior under the sponson, hold a total fuel capacity of 200 liters and provide a cruising range of up to 450 km at a speed of 64km/h. As the fuel tanks are located outside the armored hull, they don't adversely affect the vehicle's armor protection if damaged by small arms fire or shrapnel.

This M1126 Stryker Infantry Carrier Vehicle was seen at Range 307 during a blank firing exercise. On order of Captain Gentile, two M1126 Stryker ICV moved into Support by Fire Position 1 (SBF 1) where they opened fire on targets appearing at ranges up to 1,500m. The Stryker's ammunition basic load includes either 2,000 rounds of 12.7mm ammunition for the M2 HB machine gun or 480 40mm grenades for the Mk19 MOD3 automatic grenade launcher as well as sixteen 66mm smoke grenades.

consisting of a vehicle commander and a driver. These mounted crews provide critical support to the platoon by operating and maintaining the ICVs and properly employing them on the battlefield to ensure protected delivery of the infantry squads to their dismount point. Once the infantry squads have dismounted the ICVs, the vehicle crew may employ local defensive armament to defeat "thin-skinned" enemy vehicles or dismounted infantry. The infantry rifle platoon has three 9-man rifle squads and one 7-man weapons squad. These squads are at the center of the Stryker Brigade Combat Team infantry rifle platoon concept. The rifle squad is the fundamental fighting element of the rifle platoon. It is organized into two fire teams which are commanded by a squad leader. The rifle squad has nine soldiers, the squad leader, two fire team leaders, two automatic riflemen, two riflemen and two grenadiers. Their armament consists of five 5.56mm M4A1 carbines, two M4A1 carbines with 40mm M203A1 grenade launchers and two 5.56mm M249 Squad Automatic Weapons. The weapons squad consists of a squad leader and two 3-man machine gun teams. It provides the primary base for the platoon's rifle squads maneuver with highly accurate short and long range direct and small-arms fires against enemy personnel and equipment. Each of the two machine gun teams consists of a gunner, assistant gunner and ammunition bearer equipped with one 7.62mm M240B machine gun and two 5.56mm M4A1 carbines respectively.

As the M1128 Stryker Mobile Gun System (MGS) was only recently introduced into the U.S. Army on 15 May 2006, the MGS platoons of the 2nd Stryker Cavalry Regiment currently consist of two M1126 Stryker ICV and a M1134 Stryker Anti-Tank Guided Missile Vehicle (ATGM). In the future, all MGS platoons will be equipped with three M1128 Stryker MGS. Direct fire support from the MGS focuses on defeating hardened and fortified positions. The MGS features a 105 mm cannon, cal.50 machine gun in the vehicle commander's hatch, coaxial 7.62mm M240B machine gun and is designed to support the infantry with a gun that can blast through walls, knock out a fortified sniper nests, stop another armored vehicle and clear a street of enemy fighters. The MGS will carry four types of ammunition: depleted-uranium armor-piercing, high-explosive anti-tank, high-explosive plastic for blowing through walls and barricades, and a canister round filled with 2,300 tungsten ball bearings for use against dismounted enemy soldiers. The main challenges during MGS development were: producing a reliable mechanism to automatically load rounds into the cannon, an accurate stabilization system for the wheeled

The Protector M151 Remote Weapon Station (RWS) in detail. In the middle you see the Thermal Imaging Module (TIM) with the Video Imaging Module above it. Depending on mission requirements, the RWS can be fitted with either a 40mm Mk19 MOD3 automatic grenade launcher or a 12.7mm M2 HB machine gun in its universal soft-mount cradle. Four M6 smoke grenade dischargers are fitted to the RWS. Each M6 has four 66 mm barrels that can be fired simultaneously or individually.

This M1126 Stryker ICV belongs to the 2nd Platoon of Eagle Company 2-2 SCR and is armed with a 40mm Mk19 MOD3 automatic grenade launcher which can be used against slow-moving, hovering, or low-flying rotary-wing aircraft; dismounted Infantry; and lightly-armored vehicles. It automatically fires from the open-bolt position, is belt fed, blowback operated, and air-cooled.

From the commander's seat you find the RWS Fire Control Unit (FCU), with its black/white monitor, radio intercom control box and AN/PSN-11 PLGR/DAGR, to your front while the AN/VDR-2 radiacmeter, RWS control grip and part of the fire suppression system is located to your right. The FCU displays the Remote Weapon Station view as well as that of the Driver's Vision Enhancer. The vehicle commander's FBCB2 monitor is mounted to the left of the FCU in the commander's direct field of view.

The M1132 Stryker Engineer Squad Vehicle used by the 2 SCR engineer company is almost identical with the M1126 Stryker ICV, but is adapted for the storing and fitting of engineer mission specific equipment. The Jettison Fitting Kit (JFK), mounted at the lower front of the vehicles, is basically an adapter with electrical and hydraulic power connectors that allow the vehicle to be fitted with a Surface Mine Plow (SMP), an Angled Mine Plow (AMP), a Lightweight Mine Roller (LWMR) or the Straight Obstacle Blade (SOB). This 3rd Squad vehicle is equipped with the AMP, produced by Pearson Engineering, and is used to clear surface laid mines and munitions ahead of the vehicle for rapid route and area clearance operations.

A Lane Marking System (LMS) dispenser unit is mounted to the rear left and right side of the M1132 Stryker ESV. Marking intervals are set via the control box located in front of the squad leader's seat. With the LMS, a cleared lane is marked by 1,000mm long marker poles that are shot down into the surface with an air pressure of 100psi. While the standard pole is fitted with fluorescent and reflective identification panels, other poles are available with LED or IR beacons. Each electro-pneumatic LMS dispenser unit carries 50 reusable marker poles. The dispenser unit, which is reloaded manually, has a weight of 76kg, not including the marker poles and special equipment.

The 1,435kg Angled Mine Plow (AMP) removes air or artillery-delivered scatterable mines, unexploded bomblets, surface laid mines and other surface munitions, clearing a lane of approximately 3.87m wide over a variety of terrain. Like the SMP also the AMP can be fitted with the Magnetic Signature Duplicator. The AMP consists of the chassis including two three blade carriers, six blade chassis extension, ten blade carrier, left side blade extension, a hydraulic accumulator, mounting plate, boom assembly, link frame, lift cylinder, disturber chains and driving aids. The AMP with outer blades stowed for transport is 2.88m wide. Lifting the AMP takes 7 seconds and lowering with lift cylinder takes 4 seconds.

vehicle, and keeping the vehicle light enough to meet the Army's weight limitation. The gun is loaded by an automatic hydraulic handler and carries up to 18 rounds. The computerized fire-control system is virtually the same as that used in the Army's main battle tank, the M1 Abrams. The gunner and the vehicle commander track targets on computer screens inside their turret hatches. The Army eventually plans to buy a set of 27 MGSs for each of its seven Stryker brigades, at a cost of approximately $3.7 million per vehicle. The infantry company also employs a three-man sniper team consisting of a sniper, observer and one soldier securing the team. The senior man in the team is the observer, next is the sniper, and the junior man secures the sniper team. The team is capable of providing the company with a full range of sniper support and is equipped with both the 7.62mm M24 Sniper Weapons System and cal.50 M107 Long Range Sniper Rifle. The third man is armed with a 5.56mm M4A1 carbine with an attached 40mm M203A1 grenade launcher. The mortar section is the rifle company's primary indirect fire support element. The section consists of ten soldiers organized into two mortar crews each equipped with a 120mm mortar mounted on a M1129 Stryker MCV-B allowing for rapid and flexible delivery of indirect fires and increased responsiveness through rapid maneuver in support of company operations. Both crews are also equipped with a 60mm M224 Lightweight Company Mortar System which enables the section to provide a more lightweight dismounted mortar system to meet the requirements of a traditional light infantry mission. With the exception of having two mortar systems rather than four, the mortar section provides the company commander with the same indirect fire capabilities that the battalion mortar platoon provides to the battalion commander. The man-portable nature of the mortar systems gives the company commander a flexible and robust indirect fire capability. Due to crew limitations, only one system (60mm or 120mm) can be employed at a given time. Each rifle company also receives a Fire Support Team (FIST) from the HHCs Fire Support Platoon consisting of the Fire Support Officer, Fire Support NCO, Fire Support Specialist, Radio Telephone Operator and Driver. It is equipped with the M1131 Stryker FSV providing a combat laser designation capability for delivery of precision artillery or aerial-delivered munitions. The FIST assists the company commander in planning, integrating, coordinating, and executing all types of available supporting fires during tactical operations. Furthermore, the Fire Support Officer is the commander's primary fire support coordinator and provides the commander a direct link to battalion indirect fire support systems. Last but not least, a medical evacuation team with M1133 Stryker MEV from the squadron medical platoon is normally placed in direct support of each of the three infantry companies. This team has a senior trauma specialist, a trauma specialist and a driver who assist the company medical personnel with treatment and medical evacuations of ill, injured, or wounded company personnel. If required, the ambulance team provides medical evacuation of company personnel from platoon and company casualty collection points (CCP) to a supporting treatment team or to the battalion aid station (BAS) **(Graphic 5)**.

Graphic 5

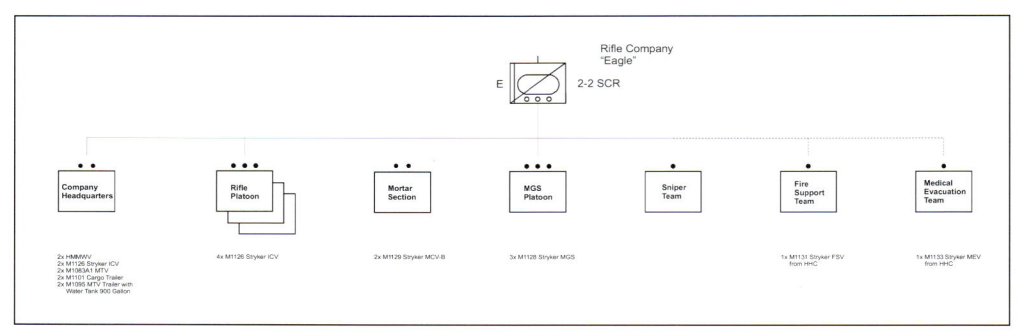

This M1132 Stryker Engineer Squad Vehicle commander was already issued the new Army Combat Uniform and the Interceptor Body Armor (IBA) in the Universal Digital Camouflage Pattern. The commander's station is located directly behind the engine compartment on the right side of the hull. There is a slightly raised, circular, single-piece hatch surrounded by seven M17E4 periscopes which provides nearly 360° visibility in the roof above the vehicle commander's seat.

The Light Weight Mine Roller (LWMR) attached to this M1132 Stryker ESV is used to detonate and neutralize buried, pressure-fused mines and other explosive devices in the vehicles path. The LWMR has a clearing width of 3,140mm with an uncleared 1,190mm center section. Main components of the LWMR are the two suspended castor roller assemblies containing four steel rollers each. The assemblies each provide approximately 400kg of ground pressure resulting in the detonation of mines before the vehicle reaches them. The roller assemblies can be quickly exchanged when damaged. Two indicator rods mounted on the outer corners of the LWMR make it easier for the driver to visualize the dimensions of the device during operation.

Magnetic Signature Duplicators, looking like black tubes, add an additional layer of mine protection to the SMP and LWMR by replicating the effects required to detonate magnetically fused mines ahead of the mechanical clearance device. This stand-off capability prevents the mechanical devices from being damaged and becoming unserviceable. The MSD has a weight of 180kg and is powered via the vehicle's 24 volt electrical system.

The regimental anti-armor company "Killer", normally attached to the 2nd Squadron, 2nd Stryker Cavalry Regiment, provides anti-tank fires and fires for breaching to support infantry assaults and destroy enemy bunkered in hard structures. On order, Killer Company mobilizes and deploys to a theater of operations and conducts area security operations within a defined area of responsibility, denying threat forces the ability to conduct consolidated attacks against coalition forces simultaneously assisting in the establishment/maintenance of a safe and secure environment for interim coalition and civil authorities to establishment/maintain a legitimate and operational government. The company is organized into a headquarters section, three anti-armor platoons, fire support platoon and a combat medic section. The headquarters section has two M1126 Stryker ICV for the company commander and his executive officer, two M1083A1 MTV trucks and two M1095 MTV trailers, one fitted with a 900 gallon water tank. Each anti-armor platoon consists of three M1134 Stryker Anti-Tank Guided Missile Vehicles (ATGM) equipped with the TOW-2B ATGM and 7.62mm M240B machine gun. The fire support platoon has a single M1131 Stryker FSV **(Graphic 6)**.

Graphic 6

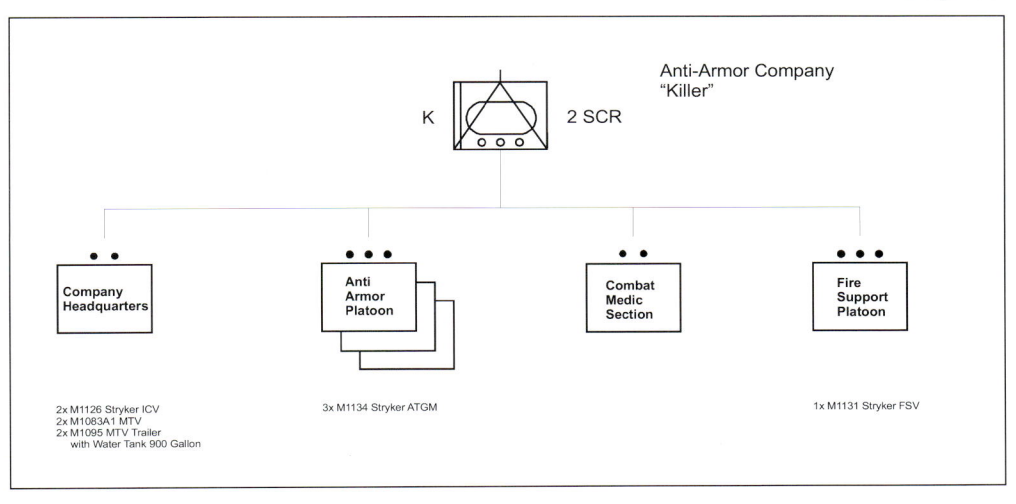

This photo shows two Eagle Company snipers wearing their Gillie suits in front of an M1126 Stryker ICV. The sniper is armed with the 7.62mm M24 Sniper Weapons System while his spotter has a 5.56mm M4A1 carbine with an attached 40mm M203A1 grenade launcher. Note that both weapons are airbrushed with camouflage paint to better blend with the environment.

The 1,260kg Straight Obstacle Blade (SOB) provides the M1132 Stryker ESV with a light earthmoving and obstacle reduction capability. It can be used to prepare defensive positions, level ground, remove urban road blocks and obstacles, fill craters, breach enemy defense positions and open routes.

The 3,000mm wide and 1,170mm high blade of the SOB is fitted with hardened steel cutting edges. Additionally, the SOB features an energy absorption mechanism protecting the blade and vehicle against damage from excessive force such as driving into an obstacle at high speed. When not in use, the compact blade is raised and stowed close to the vehicle's hull.

A view inside the troop compartment of a M1132 Stryker Engineer Squad Vehicle. The nine fully equipped soldiers enter and leave the troop compartment in the rear of the vehicle through a large power-operated rear ramp. The inward-facing bench seats on either side of the troop compartment provide seating for four soldiers on the right and five on the left. The squad leader sits on the forward end of the left bench parallel to the vehicle commander. During FTX Cougar Steel, the engineer squads only consisted of five soldiers.

The SBCT infantry company employs a three-man sniper team consisting of a sniper, observer and one soldier securing the team. The senior man in the team is the observer, next is the sniper, and the junior man secures the sniper team. The team is capable of providing the company with a full range of sniper support and is equipped with both the 7.62mm M24 Sniper Weapons System and cal.50 M107 Long Range Sniper Rifle. The third man is armed with a 5.56mm M4A1 carbine with an attached 40mm M203A1 grenade launcher.

One of the key factors of the SBCT doctrine is that the Stryker IAV equipped units can be deployed rapidly everywhere in the world within 96 hours. Due to its combat weight a single Stryker IAV is operational deployable in a C-130J Hercules cargo aircraft. On the strategic side a C-17 Globemaster III can airlift three Stryker IAV and a C-5B Galaxy can lift up to four vehicles. Depending on the future security situation in Iraq the 2nd Stryker Cavalry Regiment might get deployed in order to support Operation Iraqi Freedom by 2008 or maybe earlier. Furthermore there are plans to deploy one squadron of the 2 SCR to an Eastern Europe country. As the soldiers would be deployed without their families the squadrons would rotate every six months.

Acknowledgement:
For the outstanding support, sometimes supplied at very short notice, during research for this publication, I would like to thank Lieutenant Colonel Reineke, Lieutenant Colonel Denny, Major Oskey, Major Soika, Captain Boone, Captain Gentile, Captain Ryan, 1LT Naparstek, 1LT Santarosa, Command Sergeant Major Wood, Sergeant Major Dyckman, Mr. Damario, Mr. Dirkse, Mr. Zeilmann and the soldiers of the 2nd Stryker Cavalry Regiment "Dragoons".

Additional thanks for to Chaplain Botsford and Sergeant Pena for sharing their room with me during Field Training Exercise "Cougar Steel" in December 2006.

I would especially like to thank Captain Kenney and Captain Cox for their outstanding support and friendship helping to write this detailed report about the "Cougars".

Rock n Roll – weapons squad soldiers provide fire support while dismounted infantry soldiers attack the insurgents' hideout. The weapons squad consists of a squad leader and two 3-man machine gun teams. It provides the primary base for the platoon's rifle squads maneuver with highly accurate short and long range direct and small-arms fires against enemy personnel and equipment.

Sergeant Roberts, E/2-2 SCR's sniper, engages a target at Range 307 with his 12.9kg cal.50 M107 Long Range Sniper Rifle (LRSR). The M107 is a semi-automatic, air-cooled, box magazine-fed rifle operated by means of the short recoil principle rather than gas. The basic M107 LRSR, which has a maximum effective range against hard targets of 1,800m, is equipped with bipod, muzzle brake, carrying handle and 10-round removable magazine.

This M1129 Stryker Mortar Carrier Vehicle Version B (MCV-B) provided 120mm mortar fire support while Eagle Company soldiers engaged the insurgents on the outskirts of Dibus. The MCV-B mounts a 120mm Recoil Mortar System RMS6-L that fires a full family of mortar ammunition (HE, illumination, IR illumination, smoke, precision guided, and dual purpose improve conventional munitions).

The M95 Mortar Fire Control System (MFCS) provides a complete, fully-integrated, digital, on-board fire control system for the RMS6L 120mm mortar. The MFCS is an automated fire control system designed to provide improvements in command and control of mortar fires and the speed of employment, accuracy, and survivability of mortars.

The mortar section is the rifle company's primary indirect fire support element. The section consists of ten soldiers organized into two mortar crews each equipped with a 120mm mortar mounted on a M1129 Stryker MCV-B allowing for rapid and flexible delivery of indirect fires and increased responsiveness through rapid maneuver in support of company operations. Both crews are also equipped with a 60mm M224 Lightweight Company Mortar System which enables the section to provide a more lightweight dismounted mortar system to meet the requirements of a traditional light infantry mission.

The 1,466 lb RMS6L has a maximum rate of fire of 16 rounds per minutes and a sustained rate of 4 rounds per minutes. The company mortar carries 48 120mm rounds and 77 60mm rounds in special racks located at the side of the rear compartment. The mortar has a smooth bore with rounded muzzle to allow for easy loading. The maximum range is 7,200m while the minimum range is approximately 180m.

The 2nd Platoon entry force, consisting of an infantry squad, prepares to enter a building occupied by insurgents. They are armed with 5.56mm M4A1 carbines, 40mm M230A1 grenade launchers and a 5.56mm M249 Squad Automatic Weapon. Note the second soldier from the right carrying a tactical extrication device in a large bag.

While two infantry soldiers have M68 Close Combat Optics on their M4A1 carbines, the second trooper from the front has an EOTech Holographic Weapon Sight. As the 2nd Squadron, 2nd Stryker Cavalry Regiment hasn't received the Rapid Fielding Initiative (RFI) equipment at this time, soldiers wear a mix of DCU, ACU and Woodland camouflaged equipment. When issued RFI equipment, the soldiers will only wear ACU camouflaged uniforms and equipment.

After blowing open the door, the infantry soldiers of 2nd Platoon, Eagle company, 2-2 SCR entered the building, searched the rooms one by one and killed or arrested all insurgents. Senior NCOs and officers supervised all actions on the training lane and sometimes required certain training aspects be repeated if they weren't conducted 100% correct the first time.

A combat medic and several other troopers treat a wounded comrade during the fire-fight with the insurgents. Combat medics are trained soldiers responsible for providing first aid and frontline trauma care on the battlefield. Each rifle company has a Medical Evacuation Team with a M1133 Stryker MEV attached from the HHC Medical Platoon.

The soldiers cleared the house room by room from the first floor to the second floor. In order to prevent friendly fire inside the very narrow and complex building, soldiers yelled a short password and would not enter the next building or the room until they heard the response from their comrades.

All operations in the house occupied by the insurgents were conducted with the help of night vision goggles. 1LT Santarosa wears the AN/PVS-14 which is a lightweight, multipurpose, monocular night vision device. The objective and eyepiece assemblies allow attachment of accessories. The system features a projected IR, light-emitting diode for short range illumination for activities such as map reading. The AN/PVS-14 is supplied with the military head strap for hands-free use but most soldiers attach it directly to their helmet mounts. It allows the user complete freedom of movement while maintaining equilibrium in hands-free application. If not used, the NVGs can be fold back to the top of the helmet.

Sometimes the soldiers used Surefire flashlights, which are attached to their M4A1 Carbines, instead of their night vision goggles. The flashlight shown in this photo is a M600A Scout Light. An extremely rugged and powerful LED module produces 100 lumens of electronically-regulated light with a total runtime of nearly three hours. Switching is accomplished with a momentary-on remote tape switch that can be unplugged from the light if repairs or adjustments are required.

This M1129 Stryker MCV-B vehicle commander wears AN/PVS-7B night vision goggles while pulling security with the 7.62mm M240B machine gun mounted in his cupola. The NVG's housing is shock-resistant and sealed from the environment. With the use of a single Generation 3 image tube and a dual eye configuration, the AN/PVS-7B provides an outstanding performance-to-cost ratio.

The battalion mortar platoon in action during a raid in Riyahd. The crews used their Night Vision Goggles as well as the vehicle driver's vision enhancer to prevent detection by the insurgents.

NORWAY'S TELEMARK BATTALION
Yves Debay

From the assembly area, CV9030 of the Mechanized Company starts a combat patrol to deter any actions by insurgents.

Norwegians have a reputation for being good sailors, and despite the fame of their Viking ancestors, Norway's present-day soldiers are not so well known by the public. Nevertheless, in April 1940, Norwegian soldiers fighting side by side with British and French soldiers landed at Narvik and imposed a first defeat on the Wehrmacht. Since then a lot of water has "flowed through the fjords", and today Norway's soldiers are especially well recognized for their participation in peacekeeping missions.

During the Cold War, Norway (the only NATO member country that shared a common border with the USSR, that border being north of the polar circle) needed to rely on Allied reinforcements to assure a credible defense. Several times a year, NATO forces landed in the north of Norway to support the small but strikingly well-equipped Norwegian Armed Forces during large arctic maneuvers. The scenario was practically the same in every exercise - to counter any offensive of the Red Army based in Murmansk District. In the event of a war, Soviet units would most certainly have dashed towards the west to allow its large Northern Fleet to take to the sea.

With the implosion of the Warsaw Pact, the communist threat has all but disappeared, and all the various NATO armies as well as the *Haeren* (Norwegian Army) have experienced a decrease in size and a crisis of existence. The HQ staff in Oslo quickly became aware of these big strategic changes in the 1990s, and was swift to anticipate new strategic doctrines when it created a Norwegian rapid reaction force. In keeping with the size of Norway – it is a large country populated by only 4.3 million inhabitants – this force was to be small but extremely well equipped.

Good light soldiers serving the Danish crown
This rapid reaction force, the Telemark Battalion, was born in 1994.

Mercedes Wolf 4x4 vehicles of the Mechanized Company are seen during the first part of Exercise "Iron Sword" when the battalion was gathered in an assembly area.

Within the Mechanized Company, the Combat Platoon has four CV90 armored Infantry Fighting Vehicles (IFVs) and four Wolf vehicles.

These Wolf vehicles are armed with an MG-3 machine gun. The one behind was probably used in Afghanistan going by its sand-colored camouflage.

Telemark is in fact the name of a province in the center of Norway. This is where, in WWII, the "heavy water battle" took place, as the Norwegian resistance stubbornly fought and sacrificed to prevent the Nazis and Third Reich from developing and possessing nuclear weapons. Furthermore, in Scandinavian history, the inhabitants of Telemark supplied good-quality light soldiers to the crown of Denmark in its war against the Swedes[1].

Basically, the newly created Telemark Battalion consisted of conscripts under contract, and it was qualified to serve as a small-scale force of fast action. Unity was created under the shape of a battalion of light infantry mounted in 6x6 SISU Patria APCs.

Characterized and handicapped by a "vagueness legacy", the new unit did not participate in the entry of NATO forces into Kosovo in 1999. Even though SHAPE was counting on the Norwegians, the battalion only appeared two months after the Alliance entered the Serbian province. To prevent such a recurrence, the Norwegian parliament voted in 2002 to recreate the Telemark Battalion as a completely professional force intended to act as the Norwegian Army's rapid reaction force at the immediate disposal of NATO. The reformed unit is now known as Norwegian Army High Readiness Force (NOA HRF). To give some "punch" to the unit, the Telemark Battalion was transformed into a mechanized battalion and it became one of the nation's elite units, with 450 soldiers wearing the emerald green beret.

1. During the 16th and 17th centuries, Norway and Denmark were part of the same realm.

According to the philosophy of Norway and other European countries, a rapid intervention mechanized battalion has the same reputation as shock troops such as paratroopers, marines or the French Foreign Legion. Everything has been carefully designed so that Telemark can henceforth become the iron lance of the *Haeren*. The unit stresses the power of shock, and it has accelerated the availability and professionalism of its soldiers through intense training and delivery of the best equipment.

Ready for hand-to-hand fighting or distributing rations to children

The Telemark Battalion is trained and equipped for international operations or for policing a major national crisis. However, with the exception of a major natural disaster, there is little chance that this quiet Scandinavian country will experience such a situation within its own borders. From January to August 2005, the unit was attached as an immediately available

Belonging to the Combat Service & Support Company, the Reconnaissance Platoon is the eyes of the colonel commanding the Telemark Battalion. Two are in sand-colored camouflage and two are in olive drab. Note that two are armed with .50-cal machine guns and the other two have an MG-3. Observe also the protective grill over the windscreen.

The Reconnaissance Platoon consists of four Wolf vehicles, one of which is seen here during an intervention as part of "Iron Sword".

Machine gunners and Wolf crews in action.

combat force for the Dutch 43rd Mechanized Brigade in charge of the NATO Response Force (NRF).

As part of this responsibility, the battalion sent one of its companies to Afghanistan for the second time. Between 2003 and 2004, two companies were deployed to Kabul, where the unit suffered its first casualties during an RPG attack. The Telemark Battalion has proven it is capable of successfully completing a whole specter of missions, including serving as a conventional mechanized unit with the NRF in medium-intensity conflicts such as the one in Afghanistan.

Norwegians are in tune with Mother Nature and protect the environment well. For this reason they use red plastic blank munitions, in place of copper originals. The automatic pistol is a 9mm Glock.

This young soldier armed with a Heckler & Koch MP5 submachine-gun wears the emerald green beret that identifies this elite unit of the Norwegian Army.

Other missions assigned to the battalion are civil assistance in the case of a humanitarian disaster, peacekeeping, reinforcement and multi-lateral missions, as well as high-intensity combat operations. The following information details the unit's reaction times:
- 15 days for an NRF-type operation
- 30 days for a major operation under the command of the UN, EU or OSCE command

Lieutenant Colonel Odin Johannessen, who gave a remarkable briefing on the unit while in a staging position in the depths of a boreal forest during "Iron Sword 2005," stated: "Our 153 officers and executives, and 296 grenadiers can take a house, clearing it room by room with grenades and hand-to-hand fighting, and then distribute rations to child victims of an earthquake."

Two German Shepherds (named Billie and Oscar) serve in the Combat Service & Support Company. They are used to sniff for explosives or to find dead bodies if necessary. They could also be used in an anti-riot situation.

Here, Billie is seen during an explosives search training exercise.

When one examines the organizational chart of the Telemark Battalion, one thing is clear - it is much more than a simple mechanized infantry battalion. Telemark is a genuine task force where every specialty and all associated equipment is represented (refer to the organizational chart). This may be a nightmare for a logistician, but as long as Norway has petroleum in the North Sea, the country will be able to offer its soldiers good equipment. In the unit, the remarkable CV90 serves alongside the Leopard 2A4, Leguan bridge-layer, M113 and quad bikes. The battalion includes a Command Company, a Mechanized Company, a Tank Company endowed with the Leopard 2A4 (the only such tanks in the Norwegian Army), a Combat Engineer Company, and a Combat Service & Support Company.

A more complex organization

The spearhead of the battalion is naturally composed of the Tank Company. One finds 14 Leopard 2A4 tanks from stocks of the Dutch Army distributed in three platoons of four tanks, plus one more vehicle for the company commander and one for his second-in-command. For the moment, these Leopards are the only ones in the *Haeren*. Other Norwegian armored units are equipped with the Leopard 1A5N, a tank judged to be better adapted for arctic conditions in the north. It is important to remember that Telemark was formed for external interventions. Other vehicles found in the unit include M113 command vehicles, logistics trucks and the 4x4 Wolf for reconnaissance.

The main combat unit of the Telemark Battalion is the Mechanized Company, whose primary fighting machine is the CV9030. It has three platoons each with four CV90 vehicles. Two of these platoons are joined by four Wolf scout vehicles fitted with a 12.7mm machine gun. Of course, there are also the traditional light trucks, and logistics trucks designed to carry containers. It is noticeable that every company, with the exception of the Combat Engineer Company, is supported by a container-carrying truck in which are stored ammunition and spare parts. Besides the CV90 of the commander, the Command Platoon also has a command M113, a reconnaissance Wolf and a liaison Wolf.

The Combat Engineer Company can be considered as symbolic of the contemporary evolution of intervention units; this is because the engineers are directly integrated into the mechanized combat unit. These are pure combat engineers, those "courageous fellows" trained especially in opening breaches in enemy defenses. At the same time, the company practices identifying, clearing and creating obstacles. Derivatives of the Leopard fulfill this function with three types of vehicles based on the Leopard hull. Specifically, these include four Pioneer Panzer, two Bergepanzer that can be fitted with plows or rollers for mine clearance, and three Leguan bridge-layers. There is also a platoon of four M113 engineer vehicles, and two Fuchs for identifying NBC threats, these latter vehicles being the only ones in the Norwegian Army. Additionally, there are three quad bikes and three snowmobiles, whose mission is to "sniff" for mines or enemy obstacles in difficult terrain. Scania trucks and Wolf 4x4 vehicles complete the equipment list of the company.

The last company is the CSS (Combat Service & Support), and here a wealth of different vehicles makes this company rather unique. The commander administers various platoons that have tasks as diverse as the vehicles they operate. There is a Reconnaissance Platoon with four CV90s, four Light Terrain Vehicles (i.e. the famous Wolf armed with a .50-cal machine gun), one M113, three quad bikes and three snowmobiles. Six further quads and six snowmobiles can be activated in a platoon

The Tank Company has an M113 that can be used for command and control. It carries several soldiers charged with guarding the platoon bivouac, as seen here. Note the three-color camouflage of the M113.

The M113 machine gunner protecting the staging area of the Tank Company happens to be a young, pretty girl.

Before action, the Leopard 2A4s of the Tank Company are positioned in their assembly area in the middle of the forest. The tank seen here is "122", signifying "1" for the tank company, "2" for the 2nd platoon, and "2" for the second tank in the platoon.

commanded from two M113s, in what could be described as an intervention and scout platoon for missions in harsh terrain. FAC (Forward Air Control) specialists capable of not only guiding air attacks but also adjusting artillery fire can also be found in the CSS Company.

The doctors and medics can erect three first aid posts with their two M577 vehicles, one M113, two SISU Patria ambulances, and one Mercedes Wolf. Fire support missions occur courtesy of six M113 Mortar Carriers equipped with the British L16 81mm mortar. The company also includes a Maintenance Platoon with two Bergepanzer Leopard 1 vehicles, a Logistics Platoon with eight trucks carrying containers, two Scania trucks, and a HAT (Heavy Armor Transport) Platoon with four Scania trucks. In other words, with 13 different vehicles, the commander, his second-in-command, and his logistics NCO, have to be very competent to lead and administer the CSS.

Every company has its own colored shoulder stripes – yellow for the Mechanized Company, blue for the Tank Company, white for the CSS, and black for the Combat Engineer Company. It is the same for markings registered on some of the armored vehicles, with "1" for tanks, "3" for the mechanized section, "5" for the CSS, and "8" for the engineers.

The Telemark "man"

If the battalion is strikingly well equipped and can face a plethora of situations, its real strength remains its human elements. In this quiet and peace-loving country, those young men assigned to Telemark will have few opportunities to pick up girls in Oslo dance bars! In fact, the members are particularly well regarded by the population. First of all, these men are grenadiers in northern Europe, and that means something. It is first necessary to serve as a conscript for 12 months[2] in a regular unit before applying for a place in the TMBN (Telemark Battalion). Furthermore, places are rare.

The pay is good, with 70% of the grenadiers being graduates from Norwegian high schools. The signed contract is for between one and six years, and the average age of its members is 25 years old. With the exception of officers and NCOs, the oldest corporals do not exceed 35 years. The privates can complete courses that allow them to train in skills that will be useful in civilian life and they can also volunteer to join officers' classes. Every soldier in the Telemark Battalion must be capable of conducting high-intensity combat. He must be able to perform crowd control and maintain law and order. He must be able to assume escort missions and weapon searches. Other indispensable specialties are helicopter insertions, plus all regular tasks commonly assigned to light infantrymen.

One of the strengths of Telemark is its capacity for integration. Lieutenant Colonel Odin Johannsessen again: "90% of our soldiers have overseas

---

2. Its low population density requires Norway to retain a conscription system to feed the needs of its armed forces.

experience in the Balkans or Afghanistan. Young recruits (called "rookies" in NATO slang) are mixed in with veterans in the platoons from the time of their arrival. Selection is hard and we retain only one candidate in five. On the Norwegian scale this is a lot because the density of the population is so low. Many fail during the course of arctic survival, but if one can endure the winter conditions, then one is capable of enduring any type of conditions anywhere in the world.

Contrary to medieval legends, the Vikings were not merely fearsome warriors intent on looting. They were also merchants and curious people who liked to see the rest of the world. It is with a little bit of this outlook on life that soldiers of the Telemark Battalion esteem the Drakkar[3] badge of their prestigious ancestors.

3. Drakkar is the Norwegian name for a Viking longshi.

The organization of the unit follows that of a standard NATO tank company with three platoons of four tanks, plus two tanks for the commander and his second-in-command.

"191A", which is the call sign of the commander's tank, gives a short mobility demonstration.

The 14 Leopard 2A4 tanks of the Tank Company are seen at a staging area for maintenance operations. Note that all tanks are painted in overall olive drab camouflage. Some have a little Norwegian flag on the rear of the turret.

A Bergepanzer recovery tank based on the Leopard 1 chassis belonging to the CSS Company. Vehicles are painted in a typical three-color splinter camouflage scheme.

The Leopard 2A4 tanks of the Telemark Battalion are the only ones in service with the Haeren, and they came from Dutch Army stocks.

Note the typical Dutch smoke launchers that are different to German ones, as well as the MAG machine gun on the turret. The Norwegian Army is normally equipped with the MG-3, but as in Austria, the MAG was retained as a tank machine gun on the Leopard 2A4.

Observe the protective cover over the engine exhaust grill, this being used in winter to reduce the thermal signature of the tank. Norwegian armored vehicles are often equipped with electrical systems in place of hydraulic ones to avoid the problem of freezing when the vehicle is used north of the Arctic Circle.

Interesting side view of a Bergepanzer of the CSS in the assembly area, with a CV9030 in the background.

Various vehicles of the CSS, including CV90 IFVs of the Mechanized Company, are transported by Scania heavy trucks to their combat assembly area.

After being transported by Scania tank transporters, CV9030 IFVs are debussed in a deep forest that provides good overhead cover to the armored formation before it engages in action.

A platoon of four CV9030 IFVs is seen on a farm. Vehicles are ready for a fast intervention in a non-war/non-peace type of scenario that characterized Exercise "Iron Sword 2005."

The CV9030 is the Norwegian version armed with a 35mm automatic gun. Actually, the CV90 has been adopted by the Swedish, Swiss, Finnish, Norwegian, and most recently, the Dutch Army.

To protect their assembly area, grenadiers of the Mechanized Company are patrolling and establishing a perimeter.

Nice view of a CV9030 of the Mechanized Company of the Telemark Battalion. The number "311" represents "3" for the mechanized company, "1" for the 1st platoon, and "1" for the first vehicle.

1/35 CV9040 IFV

Laurent Lecocq

From their assembly area, CV9030s of the Mechanized Company start a combat patrol to deter any actions by insurgents.

This CV9030 is the vehicle of the Mechanized Company commander, as indicated by its number "391A".

In this scenario from "Iron Sword", the funeral of a nationalist leader degenerates into a riot against NATO.

During the simulated riot, the Telemark Battalion intervened with increasing forcefulness against the rioters. Employing the CV9030 was one step in this escalation.

A CV9030 of the Telemark Battalion is seen protecting the HQ of the NATO Response Force.

A platoon of CV9030s answers the call to deter a riot.

This view is interesting because it shows three vehicles of the 3rd Platoon used to deter rioters. Note the KFOR shields.

Soldiers of the Telemark Battalion dressed in anti-riot gear with leg protection, shield, and helmet with face protection. NATO soldiers often use such equipment and tactics in Kosovo.

Soldiers of the Telemark are armed with G3 assault rifles with telescoping butts. The Norwegian Army still retains the 7.62mm x 59 NATO caliber.

In an insurrection scenario, snipers could be used in the extreme to shoot riot leaders. Here, a Telemark sharpshooter is ready to open fire with a Mauser bolt-action rifle.

Note the blank adaptor system used for exercises, and the Aimpoint scope fitted to the G3 weapon.

This SISU Patria ambulance version has seen duty in Afghanistan, as proven by its sand-colored camouflage and Arabic characters. It is part of the Medical Platoon in the CSS.

A view of another soldier of the Telemark Battalion. They are particularly well equipped.

One of the M113s of the CSS. Note the three-color camouflage scheme and the large tarpaulin stowed on the front of the vehicle.

One of the rarest vehicles used by the Telemark Battalion is this Pioneer Panzer on a Leopard 1 chassis.

Quad bikes are used by the Combat Engineer and Scout Platoons to gain access to difficult areas.

The Telemark Battalion has its own HAT (Heavy Armor Transport) with four Scania trucks.

A Scania tank transporter is seen here during the battalion's initial display phase during "Iron Sword 2005".

Even if the quality of this picture is not fantastic, it is nevertheless interesting because it shows one of the few Fuchs NBC vehicles of the battalion.

Afghanistan's Battleweary T-62 Tanks
3rd Tank Kandak

Yves Debay

"B-34" is the primary tank used for instruction. It is a T-62M with bra armor fitted around the front of the turret. The instructors have added yellow tape around some principal components of the tank, especially near the sights, for instruction purposes. The camouflage of the tank is pretty standard with a mix of dark brown, light green and sand.

Background to Afghanistan's T-62 tanks

The traveler who visits Afghanistan today will observe, in the midst of its superb landscapes, dozens of tank wrecks. These include T-34, T-54/55 and T-62 tanks without turrets or tracks, wrecks that litter the battlefields where Mujahideen, Soviet and Afghan Government soldiers, plus the Taliban, confronted each other over a period of nearly thirty years. With the exception of the Red Army and the Government forces of Babrak Karmal or Doctor Najibullah[1], which were backed by Moscow, no formal armored units have existed in the resistance. Nevertheless, tanks and BTR armored personnel carriers captured from the Soviet or Government forces were used; these included vehicles driven away by deserting soldiers.

After the capture of Kabul and the defeat of the Communists, Ahmed Shah Massoud, the Minister of Defense, reorganized the Army to include several armored units. When the capital was abandoned in 1996, the Mujahideen and Taliban used these former tanks of the Afghan Army in small quantities to support their infantry. The Mujahideen concentrated their tanks on the 30km wide and 80km long Shomali Plain north of Kabul, but they suffered from a chronic shortage of spare parts. To some extent, this was compensated for by the ingenuity of the Afghan warriors. The situation on the northern front near the town of Taloqan was even more dramatic because, in 2000, Takhar province was defended by about ten "out-of-breath" T-55 tanks only. The Taliban did not know about these problems, even though they knew their opponents' equipment was old. Spare parts were usually brought from Pakistan[2] or were purchased directly from the Ukrainian mafia with the use of illicit drug money.

11 September 2001 was to upset the status quo, however. The USA, after having tried to build an "Alliance of the South" with former Pashtun Mujahideen[3] and "moderate" Taliban members (which

---

[1]. Doctor Najibullah was the former leader of KHAD (State Information Ministry), the secret Afghan Communist Police. He replaced Babrak Karmal in 1986. It is reported that he sometimes personally attended torture sessions. Though rescued by Massoud during the capture of Kabul in 1992, Najibullah was arrested and shot by the Taliban in a United Nations building, before his body was hung up in the street.

[2]. Chinese-manufactured T-59 tanks of the Pakistan Army use components that are in common with the T-55 MBT (Main Battle Tank) serving in Afghanistan.

[3]. Abdul Haq, a former Pashtun leader and hero of the fight against the Soviet Union, infiltrated the south in October 2001 with the CIA. He was arrested and hanged by the Taliban.

"B-32" is a T-62M with armor around the turret. During the Communist era, Afghanistan received 170 T-62 tanks of various versions from the Soviet Union.

"A-22" of A Company is ready to start a morning session of driver training. The T-62 was designed as a successor to the T-55 by the Kartsev Bureau Vagonka at Nizhnyl in the Soviet Union. A certain number of components in common with the T-54/55 were incorporated in the newer T-62 design, but the hull is longer and wider, and the new turret has a diameter of 2.245m instead of 1.845m for the older model.

seems to be a contradiction in terms), finally realized that the only solution would be to support the Northern Alliance, the only force capable of occupying territory on the ground. On the northern Taloqan front, the embryo of a homogenous armored force was slowly developing. A squadron of "new" T-55 tanks taken directly from Red Army stocks, and paid for in dollars, was engaged in the Kunduz campaign.

After the defeat of the Taliban in 2001, the return of "peace" brought about a process of disarmament known as DDR (Disarmament, Demobilization and Reintegration), where warlords were to hand in their heavy weapons and military materiel to ISAF (International Security Assistance Force)[4]. At the same time, a new Afghan army was to be created - it was to be known as the ANA, the Afghan National Army.

A first, and currently unique, tank battalion was created on paper in the spring of 2004 under the name of the 3rd Tank Kandak, which formed part of the 3rd Mechanized Brigade. Its equipment is quite antiquated as, at present, Afghanistan does not have the means to obtain any newer second-generation MBTs, plus it was necessary to withdraw the remainder of the armored vehicles that were still in service after more than twenty years of combat. The T-62, the most "modern" tank available in the theater, was selected to equip this new unit.

When the Soviet Union withdrew from Afghanistan in 1989, they had left behind an impressive force of tanks, of which a large number were T-62s. These T-62 tanks had fought in the wars between the Mujahideen and the new national army between 1991 and 1994. They also saw action against Gulbuddin Hekmatyar, and later against the newcomers that were known as the Taliban[5]. The Taliban seized the army's barracks during the capture of Kabul, capturing many tanks in the process. As a consequence, many T-55 and T-62 tanks were employed by the Taliban against the T-55s and T-62s of the Mujahideen on the Plain of Shomali, these latter tanks having been salvaged from the disastrous loss of Kabul. Put simply, these tanks are very run down, with some little more than rolling derelicts.

ISAF assistance

Within the framework of the training of the new ANA, Lieutenant Colonel Nassem, the former leader of Massoud's armored units, received command of the 3rd Tank Kandak. This unit was to benefit greatly from the assistance of ISAF. Romania, the only member of NATO to still operate the T-62, supplied a detachment of technical advisers, whereas Germans took charge of tactical instruction. A small American team helped with logistics and with the command cell. The Romanian Army sent six instructors to Kabul to train the drivers, and nine technicians who were put in charge of maintenance. For Germany's part, twelve specialists of the Bundeswehr Panzertruppen were assigned to teach the Afghans about the intricacies of the use of these tracked vehicles.

4. One would have liked to believe it was going to happen!

5. The Taliban consisted of religious students who formed this movement in *madrassas* (religious schools) in Pakistan. The singular is *Talib*, and the plural is *Taliban*.

Here, some American advisors are happy to receive a ride on an Afghan T-62. For older members of the U.S. Army, as well as for NATO troops, the T-62 was once considered a potential adversary from the Warsaw Pact...but times have changed!

A German instructor stands in front of "A-24", a T-62. Germans are in charge of teaching tank combat tactics to the Afghan crews, while Romanians are the technical and mechanical experts.

A platoon of infantrymen marches past a T-62 tank. It is very difficult for Western advisers to try to build an army that meets NATO standards. While the recruits and personnel have an excellent disposition for war, they do so in a peculiarly Afghan way.

"B-24" is seen during driver trials. Note that the tank does not have either lights or armor plates on the front glacis plate, the latter being used to protect against anti-tank projectiles. The original T-62 had the same engine as the T-55, though the cooling system was improved by the provision of a larger diameter fan. The suspension is similar to that on the T-55, but the mounts have been rearranged since the hull is longer.

The young and sympathetic Captain Aurel Neamtu, commander of the Romanian detachment, declared: "It was near Jalalabad in the south that we met for the first time the Afghan tank crews that had been involved in the fight against the Taliban. They had an incredible collection and mixture of machines in a state of almost total decay. To establish a unit that is up to NATO standards with this tracked "mixture" was a real challenge."

The example of engine oil is emblematic of the state of these armored vehicles. When one sees an Afghan T-55 or T-62 with its aura of black smoke, it gives the impression that it consumes more oil than fuel! With a lack of oil supplies, the Romanians asked a U.S. liaison officer to solve this problem. The officer concerned tapped on his computer and through a miracle of American organization and logistics, a C-17 Globemaster II landed in Bagram airbase one week later with a cargo consignment of engine oil. The Afghans and Romanians eagerly received a large quantity of NATO-standard oil that had little resemblance to the oil used in vehicles of the former Warsaw Pact. The Soviet engines, which are made in the Urals, do not digest at all well the delicate oil used to feed the turbines of the M1 Abrams! Poland and the Czech Republic were also to supply certain spare parts, but gifts mainly consisted of spare engine parts rather than optical equipment, of which there is a shortage. Fortunately, military vehicle wrecks abound in Afghanistan and a number of tanks could be cannibalized for spare parts.

Operational training began in the spring of 2005 with forty-four such "revitalized" tanks, with fire and movement drills taking place. The German instructors have no criticisms of the way they are operating. Though the crews of the 3rd Tank Kandak use their tanks in "an Afghan way", they still know how to shoot. This was a surprise to the Westerners. The Oberstleutnant (Lieutenant-Colonel) commanding the German instruction detachment reported: "The T-62 is not a Leclerc, nor a Leopard 2A6, that is designed to fire on the move. In our eyes, the stabilization system of the Russian tank turret is little more than rudimentary, but nonetheless, one of the gunners (a former member of the Mujahideen), hit four targets out of four with his tank on the move. This man, Noor Alah Sahev, will graduate and receive a "fine shooter" award that was especially made for him. In the meantime, all NATO safety standards are respected."

In April 2005, the 3rd Tank Kandak was ready as a NATO-standard unit with forty-four T-62 and T-62M tanks (the latter has additional armor plates), plus four recovery tanks based on the T-55 chassis. The battalion includes a Command and Support Company (which includes the tanks of Colonel Nassem and his second-in-charge), as well as three combat companies. These latter companies are organized into three platoons of

"C-66" is the tank belonging to the commander of Charlie Company. It is a T-62M version that is fitted with a Sheksna laser-guided missile system, passive armor protection, a V-55-5 engine, and the R-173 communication system. The 9K116-1 Sheksna (the NATO designation for it is AT-10 "Stabber") is probably not used actively on Afghan tanks anymore. The main armament is a stabilized 115mm smoothbore gun fitted with a bore evacuator, a feature that permits immediate visual differentiation from a T-55.

A detailed view of the front of the turret with its extra passive armor plates. The mount for the 12.7mm DshKM heavy machine gun can be seen on the loader's cupola, though the weapon itself is not fitted. The Afghan Army badge is present, as well as a Persian inscription and a Western-type code number. The three tank companies take the letters A, B and C.

"C-66" leaves the camp and negotiates a slope on its way to the range. The tank battalion's camp is situated in the southeast part of Kabul on the road towards Jalalabad. This series of pictures is interesting because it shows the main recognition features of the T-62 that help distinguish it from the older T-55. These features include a longer and wider hull, different spacing of the road wheels (with the T-62 having a distinctive gap between the third, fourth and fifth road wheels), the shape at the rear of the turret, and a longer and thicker gun barrel with its fume extractor.

four tanks each, plus a tank for the captain and his second-in-command. For the first time, a company of this new ANA armored unit did a march-past in Kabul to celebrate the national holiday on 28 April 2005.

Getting an ANA brigade operational

The main objective of the ANA is to put one operational brigade into each province, with a total force of 70,000 men under arms. It is planned that one Army Corps with three brigades will be operational in the south and east of Afghanistan, with another two brigades in the north. Kabul Central Corps will have three brigades. The 1st and 2nd Brigades are actually already operational, and the 3rd Brigade is acting as a Quick Reaction Force (QRF).

A typical ANA brigade is organized as follows:
- HQ and HQ Company
- Three Infantry Battalions
- Support Battalion with an Artillery Battery, Reconnaissance Company and Anti-Tank Company. The aforementioned Tank Battalion presented in this article is attached to the 3rd Brigade.
- Logistics Battalion with a Maintenance Company, a Transportation Company and a Signals Company

The main problem is that the ANA is being totally reformed and built at the same time as it is engaged in a war against the Taliban. This fact, and a lack of equipment, has reduced the scope of the training program. ISAF and NATO have given military assistance to the ANA in the KMTC (Kabul Military Training Center). U.S. forces are in charge of AIT (Advanced Individual Training) of the soldiers, which lasts for fourteen weeks.

The British are leading the formation of the NCO cadre, a process that takes five weeks for junior NCOs and three months for senior NCOs. Officers are being trained by the French in two ways. The first OTB (Officer Training Brigade) trained platoon leaders as lieutenants over a period of eleven weeks. The CGSC (Command General Staff College) is a course that lasts four months to train staff officers at the brigade level. The French are also training engineers. The establishment of the artillery is in the hands of a Mongolian detachment, which gives instruction on 82mm and 120mm mortars, as well as 122mm D-30 howitzers. As outlined already, the formation of the armored force is in the hands of Romanian and German personnel.

Many Afghan people possess an innate disposition for military matters and qualities, and have a real thirst for knowledge. In addition, many demonstrate a real enthusiasm for the new national army. It is equally true that getting a job as a soldier guarantees a salary in a country that is very poor, and this is also an important consideration. While some NCOs are not able to read maps, they still have a fantastic sense of terrain and topography. The accompanying photos show a small ceremony celebrating an officer promotion ceremony at the KMTC.

A general view of the battalion's motor park. Within the squadron, tanks are mixed between T-62 and T-62M models, but all are covered with the new national camouflage paint scheme of light green, brown and sand.

This view shows the long 115mm gun barrel of tank "A-24". Of the forty rounds of 115mm ammunition carried, two ready rounds are kept in the turret – one round by the gunner's feet, and one by the loader's feet. In addition, there are sixteen shells in the forward part of the tank to the right of the driver, and twenty in the rear of the fighting compartment. A 7.62mm PKT machine gun mounted coaxial to the right of the main armament has a practical rate of fire of 200-250 rounds per minute, and is fed by a belt containing 250 rounds.

These Afghan tanks were not hit by an enemy missile, but were simply starting their engines or changing gears, an action that produced a thick "smokescreen"! This is explained by the age of these tanks that have served with both sides during Afghanistan's protracted conflicts. As explained in the text, NATO engine oil was not well suited to the Russian engines.

A parked T-62. Organization of the 3rd Tank Kandak Battalion was based on a standard NATO battalion as elaborated in the accompanying text.

46

A Model V-55-5 V-12 water-cooled diesel engine with fuel injection system is being studied by the crew. The T-62's engine develops 580hp at 2,000rpm.

Four T-55 recovery vehicles are in service with the 3rd Tank Kandak. They retain their original Soviet green paint scheme.

The crew of a BRDM-2 works on the 14.5mm KPV machine gun, the weapon mounted in the turret of this famous Russian reconnaissance vehicle.

The 3rd Tank Kandak has a small reconnaissance platoon in each of its companies. This recce platoon consists of four BRDM-2 vehicles. Their camouflage scheme is similar to that found on the tanks.

An honorary company parades in front of VIPs. The officer has a ceremonial sword, and the soldiers walk with a Soviet drill style of goosestep.

A lack of suitable military transport is illustrated in these pictures, with common civilian trucks being used to carry the Afghan soldiers. This may look efficient with a full company transported in a single truck, but it might not be as efficient tactically!

In the period of Taliban rule, it was an offence to listen to music or to dance. Here, Pashtun soldiers perform a traditional warrior dance to celebrate the successful completion of their officers' course.

Soldiers are seen receiving basic training. Incredibly, they wear Romanian helmets, U.S. woodland camouflage uniforms, and carry AK-47 weapons. In the first year of its formation, the ANA was short of Kalashnikov rifles because warlords ordered their men to keep their weapons for themselves. Therefore, Romania, Bulgaria and even Russia, the former invader, sent Kalashnikov weapons to Afghanistan to help equip the fledgling army.